The TV Guide to Telling Your Organization's Story:

Insights and tools to help you navigate the Interactive Age

Megan McDonald & John Doyle

WS PRESS

WS Press
ISBN-13: 978-0615948164
ISBN-10: 0615948162

Contents

Find Your Story

Tell your story

Live your story

ACKNOWLEDGMENTS

Many thanks to our wonderful editors, Nona Allison and Cheryl Jenkins. Their efforts improved the book immeasurably, and any remaining errors are entirely ours.

The Odd Couple: A Note from the Authors

Where would you be today if, back in 1994, someone gave you a book that explained how cell phones, PCs, and tablets were going to change the world over the next two decades?

> This is that book.

No, John, it isn't. But it does serve as a primer on some of the large-scale shifts affecting communications and provides strategies that you can adopt to successfully navigate them, using the model of a TV show.

> A *TV Guide*, if you will.

And much like a *TV Guide*, it provides brief but enlightening overviews, not of shows but of concepts and tactics that you can use to tell your organization's story more effectively. It also helps you identify areas that you are interested in spending more time learning about.

> What it doesn't do is teach you how to tweet, post, #hashtag, or Skype. And if you're looking for scholarly insights about the literary themes in famous stories, you've got the wrong book.

Instead, it delivers the context and insights to help you become a better communicator in any medium.

> And it does it in a way that allows you to jump around so you're not forced to read a bunch of chapters just to get to the good parts.

Specifically, this book is comprised of four distinct sections which can be read independently or in any combination. The first section explains how we communicate with each other today—both as individuals and as organizations—and what we can do to communicate more effectively. Sections two, three, and four offer specific advice on how to successfully find, tell, and live your story in the Interactive Age.

And there are quite a few pictures and bullet points to make the reading feel a lot less like work.

One of the reasons our partnership works is that we're extremely different in our perspectives, experiences, mentalities … and writing styles. So you will notice two distinctly different voices in this book.

Hence the two different fonts.

I tend towards abstract and educational tones, while John provides concrete narratives.

The combination of two very different minds also went into the overall structure of the book. I usually read books from start to finish, and prefer a cumulative, linear approach to learning.

Blessed with the gift of attention deficit disorder and a dash of dyslexia, I like the freedom to hop in and out of a book without having to remember a lot of plot. So I need short sections, pictures and lots of white space.

Regardless of your preferred style of learning or level of background, this book will be helpful in navigating the future of communication.

And we hope you have fun reading it.

"Kinda like a 21st century *Moonlighting*, right Megan?"

"Not so much, John."

"I hate television. I hate it as much as peanuts. But I can't stop eating peanuts."

—*Orson Welles*

"If television's a babysitter, the Internet is a drunk librarian who won't shut up."

—*Dorothy Gambrell,* Cat and Girl Volume I

"The difference between TV and the internet was how far you sat from the screen. TV was an 8 foot activity, and you were a consumer. The internet was a 16 inch activity, and you participated."

—*Seth Godin*

Face the Nation: How the Internet gave the power back to the people and what that means for you

Nanny and the Professor —In 2011, part-time nanny Molly Katchpole told Bank of America CEO Brian Moynihan and the online world that she didn't want to pay a new $5 monthly debit card fee. Moynihan was "incensed by the bad press," and vowed that he "won't budge on the new fees." But the banker budged ... and the nanny won.

Hollywood Squares—In 2012, Hollywood's top lobbyist Chris Dodd blasted his former colleagues in the US Senate for killing his signature legislation, the *Stop Online Piracy Act*, which would have allowed the government to censor the Internet. Upon losing what had appeared to be a slam-dunk deal, an enraged Dodd said, "Don't ask me to write a check for you [politicians] when you think your job is at risk and then don't pay any attention to me when my job is at stake." This refreshing candor resulted in its own online petition on the White House website calling for an investigation into Dodd's alleged "open admission of bribery."

Soul Train—In 2013, Canadian PM Stephen Harper announced that he "has a lot of fun twerking," but only with close friends and "every now and then with President Obama." Before a media aide could update the PM on early 21st century parlance, he added that he "would like to twerk with every Canadian but that of course is impossible."

"That's what twerking means? Why didn't somebody tell me that *before* my speech?"

There was a time when emulating society's leaders was a viable strategy for success. But those days are truly gone.

1 **The 20ᵗʰ century leadership skills that catapulted people to positions of power—being unilaterally decisive and hogging the megaphone, to name just two—are liabilities in the Interactive Age, where collaboration trumps intimidation.**

The sense of unassailable superiority by those in power is resulting in regular digital spankings as the once-untouchable establishment titans go head-to-head with "little people" who may lack executive prerogative, but more than make up for it in social media savvy.

> *"It's a watershed event, what happened," Dodd admitted, noting that opponents' "ability to organize and communicate directly with consumers" was a game-changing phenomenon that he hadn't seen in more than three decades in public office.*
>
> *– Hollywood Reporter, January 2012*

But if successful business and political icons of the 20ᵗʰ century can no longer guide us to success, who can?

Television.

> Yup. The faithful companion that taught you how to run faster, jump higher, and build strong bodies 12 ways can now help you navigate the roiling waters of social media.

Think about it. The world is changing faster and more dramatically than at any point in human history. Every aspect of communications is changing in ways we could never have imagined a decade ago. Keeping up with the changes is next to impossible and the struggle can overwhelm the strongest of us.

One way to get grounded and to regain a sense of balance is to filter these new experiences through the lens of something familiar; something that is feeling its way through this brave new world like you are. And there's nothing more familiar and universal—in the 20th century, anyway—than television.

2 **The monolithic monologues that were the hallmark of "communication" in the 20th century have been replaced by countless dialogues—richer, more personal stories that are shared by smaller communities through an array of interactive media.**

As the television industry navigates its way through these tectonic changes, it can teach us how to respond to similar challenges. The static monologues delivered via press releases, white papers, and the vetted and sanitized "statement from the CEO" are rapidly being replaced by genuine dialogue between organizations and the audiences they want to reach.

Similarly, TV is restructuring its programs so that it can engage in a dialogue with its audiences. The signs of this restructuring are on every channel:

- Folks watching *Hawaii 5-0* can determine the ending of the program in real time by selecting the bad guy via Twitter.
- Netflix uploaded every episode of *House of Cards* to allow people to watch it when *they* choose to.
- A number of programs (including my favorite, *The Blacklist)* post Chyrons (those messages on the bottom of the screen) prompting you to download the episodes and the show's soundtrack on iTunes.
- Vine superstar Logan Paul took over the *Today Show's* Vine account … live. (Don't understand that sentence? You will.)
- CBS's *Showtime* Network partnered with LG Technologies to develop a system that allows viewers to participate in polls and trivia games about *Showtime* programs such as *Dexter* and *Ray Donovan* as they watch the shows.
- Connect TV has an app that lets viewers capture six seconds of the show they're watching and send that clip to their friends.
- The app *Viggle* identifies the show you're watching and then connects you to others watching the show via Facebook and other social media. It also allows you to rack up points for every minute

you watch the show, which can then be redeemed from the show's partners.

- Engaging TV ads are no longer restricted to the *Super Bowl* as advertisers fight for viewers' attention with better content and real-time interactivity.
- TV networks are partnering with content distribution platforms—from YouTube to Apple TV—to ensure that their programs can be viewed anywhere on myriad devices.
- Television manufacturers are taking the dialogue concept one step further with social television technology that allows you to literally talk to your television system.

Television watching has come a long way from trying to draw tires on *Winky Dink's* bicycle, and this is just the beginning.

Oscar-winning actor Kevin Spacey best summed it up when he said, "For kids growing up, there's no difference between watching *Avatar* on an iPad or watching YouTube on a TV and watching *Game of Thrones* on their computer. It's all content. It's all story."

"The audience has spoken," he said. "They want stories. … And they will engage with it with a passion and an intimacy that a blockbuster movie could only dream of—and all we have to do is give it to them."

"And after you finish drawing on the TV, I'll teach you how to play *Flying Saucer Tag* with mother's fine china!"

You don't need to invent an app to remain relevant. But you do need to share compelling stories with your audiences if you want to attract and hold their attention. And TV can show you how.

The Daily Show: Channeling your inner TV show

It's not just TV's future that will guide us. Our connection with TV's past is also very helpful. Most of us *get* TV. We were raised on it and have spent a lot of time with it. If you subscribe to the theory that 10,000 hours of practice makes a world-class expert, then most of us are TV experts. Or at least, TV-watching experts. If you're looking for a common cultural and intellectual touch-point, TV is hard to beat.

You understand the medium, and the commercialization of dependable shows delivering content that the audience values. Additionally, you understand that these shows need to be scripted, produced, and marketed. So imagining your organization as a TV show is a great exercise for thinking about the new responsibilities—and opportunities—that you now face.

3 **In using TV as your muse, the most important element is the inherent and ongoing relationship the audience has with a TV show.**

This relationship is built on an unwritten contract, which is both the good news and the bad news.

On the up side, you build trust and emotional ties with your audience. They become invested in your story.

On the other hand, you really do have to deliver on a fairly consistent basis. You aren't expected to be perfect (thank heavens), but you do need to consistently produce content in line with your audience's expectations and your contract with them … like TV shows.

> When you plop down to watch your favorite TV show, you want safe, dependable conflict. Your online audience expects the same. They've got a lot of flavors to choose from. Take the time to develop a template for your most compelling stories, and then don't veer too far from the original blueprint.

It's a fine line, however, since TV shows tell new stories every week with the same established structure. So to keep from becoming predictable, you will need to get creative.

4 Familiarity is comforting. Repetition is not. A loyal TV audience keeps coming back because they want to know "what happens next." Same goes for your online followers. You need to keep the narrative flowing and to keep your stories fresh.

The secret to keeping TV shows fresh despite formulaic plots and familiar settings is the action of the show's characters. When you sit down to watch your favorite show, you have an unspoken guarantee that your favorite characters are going to find themselves in some sort of conflict. This conflict naturally creates a tension that pulls the audience more deeply into the story.

> Strong and interesting characters keep us coming back. Sure he's an annoying, acerbic, astringent addict, but when we watch *Elementary*, we expect Sherlock Holmes to agitate us, as long as he also dazzles us with his deductive prowess.
>
> And the lovable and grossly inappropriate Michael Scott, regional manager of *The Office* (Scranton branch), made us simultaneously laugh and cringe as he unwittingly plowed through the barriers of office etiquette, decorum, and sexual harassment policy in pursuit of a smile.
>
> And *Family Guy* Peter Griffin … fuggetaboutit! He makes my *dog* cringe.
>
> On the other end of the character spectrum is *C-SPAN,* which is known for broadcasting congressional hearings and interviews with old white guys in suits. To be fair, a lot of these guys are characters. But interesting they are not. As a result, *C-SPAN's* ratings are miniscule. But they do have an impassioned audience—a plethora of policy wonks inside the Beltway— seasoned with a smattering of political junkies across North America.

Which leads us to our next point: TV shows cater to specific targeted audiences more than ever before. The nation isn't sitting down on Sunday nights at 7:30 p.m. to watch *The Wonderful World of Disney* anymore. America's TV-watching nuclear family has exploded into a hundred million little Nielsens all searching for stories that they rate worthy of watching.

5 To keep their ratings (and their spirits) up, TV producers are doing what the most popular websites do: they're identifying very specific—and usually smaller—audiences that matter most, and they're

tailoring their content to reach them.

And while TV show producers care a lot about ratings, their definition of success has expanded well beyond how many eyeballs their show can attract. More important is who those eyeballs belong to. A small impassioned audience is worth far more to advertisers than an audience chock full of anonymous eyeballs.

> Besides, ratings are relative. Tom Hanks would get *extremely loud and incredibly close* to losing it if his next movie bombs like that schmaltzy tearjerker did. (You know that movie he did, *Extremely Loud and Incredibly Close*? Anybody? Tough crowd.) But his *Bosom Buddy* Peter Scolari--the Brian Dunkleman of TV sitcoms—would be ecstatic to have that many people hate his work. (Don't know who Peter Scolari is? Exactly.)

6 **You need to constantly monitor your site's data to see what works and what doesn't—and then adjust your content accordingly.**

As in TV, your success as a content marketer and organizational storyteller is dependent on your ability to produce and deliver content that *connects* with your audience—over and over again. Your ability to receive and incorporate feedback from your audience and evolve with them is critical, too. So don't expect your story to remain the same. You need to evolve.

Launching and maintaining a successful online presence is not nearly as difficult as producing a TV series. But it will take time, collaboration, and dedication to succeed. In the end, you'll find that it's worth it.

And, frankly, what choice do you have? That's where your audience is.

"No! Don't retweet it. That's exactly what they expect us to do."

Growing Pains: Major Stages of a TV Show

Every TV show can be broken down into three broad segments: story creation, show time, and program management. The same is true for your organization.

The "let's hold a press conference next month" approach to organizational communication does not cut it in the Interactive Age.

Story creation: Finding your story

When we feel like the online revolution has marched on without us, it's tempting to jump into social media as quickly as possible, even if that means sacrificing the development of a strategy. Your boss wants to "be on that Twitter thing" but she has no idea what she wants to say, how she will integrate the workload into the staffing structure, or how she will define success. So she hands the responsibility to staff.

And hilarity inevitably ensues. Here are a couple of gems:

- An employee of New Media Strategies dropped the f-bomb in a tweet about how bad people in Detroit drive while driving from a meeting with their client, Chrysler Motors. New Media fired the employee. Chrysler fired New Media.

- The CFO at clothing retailer Francesca's tweeted great news "Board meeting. Good Numbers=Happy Board." Unfortunately, Francesca's is a publicly traded company and the CFO broke the law. "Insider Trading=Unhappy SEC."

- When an American Red Cross employee used his American Red Cross twitter account to boast that he and his buds were #gettngslizerd (sic) on beer, his boss tweeted an apology and promised to confiscate the offender's keys.

It's vital to start with a plan. Just as a TV show has a script to get everyone on the same page about who is doing and saying what at any given time, an organization needs to have a concrete story that it aims to convey. The script then becomes the blueprint for casting, props, staging, *etc.*

Show time: Telling your story

Once you've got a good handle on what you want to say, you need to figure out how to tell that story. If you can tell one good story, you can tell many. But as any cocktail party will show you, most people are abysmal storytellers. Fortunately, this is a skill that can be taught. And in a world where everyone who works for—or with—your organization has a megaphone, that training is highly worthwhile.

Program management: Living your story

7 **Just like a TV show, it takes regular and ongoing communications to make an organization's story come alive. This is not a "special project"; it is a new way of organizing and integrating your staffing to meet communications challenges that develop.**

In the following pages, we will walk you through information and tips to help you complete all three of these stages and be able to find, tell, and live your organization's story in the Interactive Age.

Land of the Giants: When They Ran the Show(s)

> Ours must be a leadership democracy, administered by the "intelligent minority" who know how to regiment and guide the masses. The common interests very largely elude public opinion entirely, and can be managed only by a specialized class whose personal interests reach beyond the locality.
>
> –*Edward Bernays*

Did you ever watch *The Little Rascals* and marvel at how different the world was back in the 1930s? Well, the late 20th century has a lot more in common with Hal Roach's universe than it does with our current world. In fact, the mass communications infrastructure that shaped the last century was set into motion before Alfalfa was a twinkle in his biological father's eye.

The 20th century was the Golden Age of managed messaging. Media moguls, corporate titans, and government agencies controlled virtually every aspect of mass communication. This "intelligent minority" were literally the "they" in any statement that began with "They say…"

The blueprints for this power paradigm were drawn up in the wee hours of the 20th century by Edward Bernays, the man who would be crowned "the father of public relations."

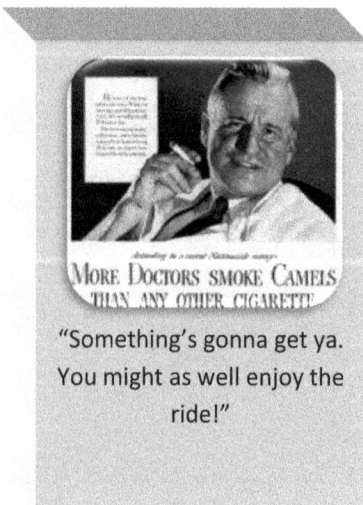

More Doctors smoke Camels than any other cigarette

"Something's gonna get ya. You might as well enjoy the ride!"

In his aptly named essay, *Propaganda*, Bernays asked, "If we understand the mechanism and motives of the group mind, is it not possible to control and regiment the masses according to our will without their knowing about it?"

Turns out it was possible … and very profitable. (A small example: It was Bernays who convinced America that women had the *right* to smoke in public with his "Torches of Freedom" campaign.)

Bernays—who was related to Sigmund Freud through both his mother (Freud's sister) and his father (whose sister married

Freud)—knew a few things about crowd psychology and other psychoanalytic approaches to public relations, which he called "the engineering of consent."

He was also keenly aware that the burgeoning mass media infrastructure of 20th century America—"this web of communications" he presciently called it—was ideal for the "manipulation of the organized habits and opinions of the masses." This was critical, he wrote, because "those who manipulate this unseen mechanism of society constitute an invisible government which is the true ruling power of our country."

America's mass media infrastructure was critical to Bernays' success in developing "technique[s] for the mass distribution of ideas." These techniques, which he collectively dubbed "public relations," were amazingly effective because they were based on the belief that "the United States has become a small room in which a single whisper is magnified thousands of times."

But the Internet destroyed that small room a few years back and countless communities have popped up in its place. The people in those communities aren't buying the linear monologues spouted by corporations, media conglomerates, and political leaders. They are putting their faith in their friends and their communities, with astounding results.

8 **Social media has brought us full circle to what Bernays described as "an earlier age … [where] a leader was usually known to his followers personally [and] communication was accomplished principally by personal announcement to an audience."**

This has up sides for organizations of all sizes, but our new reality requires that you make a few adjustments to your communications program if you want to be heard in the Interactive Age.

Public Relations has been toeing the Bernays line fairly consistently ever since. Need proof? Here is Bernays' definition of public relations, circa early 1900s:

> *Public relations is the management function that tabulates public attitudes, defines the policies, procedures, and interests of an organization followed by executing a program of action to earn public understanding and acceptance.*

Here is one of the Public Relations Society of America's three finalists in their "international effort to modernize the definition of public relations," circa 2012:

> *Public relations is the management function of researching, engaging, communicating, and collaborating with stakeholders in an ethical manner to build mutually beneficial relationships and achieve results.*

Like father, like son.

As the World Turns: Communicating in the Interactive Age

The traditions of influence in Washington, where a little pressure from a well-heeled corporate donor could help tip a debate or seal a deal, seem to have broken down.

–The Washington Post, September 2013

The transition from the Information Age (when the "intelligent" minority controlled the microphone) to the Interactive Age (where regular people like us decide what they want to talk about, and to whom) has been so swift and so decisive that we can almost hear cigars exploding in board rooms around the globe as the former Masters of the Universe frantically apply 20th century solutions to 21st century challenges.

Consider McDonald's.

Fred Turner, chairman of the board of the McDonald's fast food empire from 1977 until his retirement in 2004, was crowned "The Adman of the Decade" in the 1980s by *Advertising Age*. He was a masterful 20th century marketer. And his success was, in many ways, attributable to the storytelling elements he applied to McDonald's marketing strategy.

He identified and focused on his target audience.

As America's nuclear families radiated out to the suburbs in the 1960s, Turner directed his troops to follow them. "Our move to the suburbs was a conscious effort to go for the family business. That meant going after the kids." *–TIME,* 1973

He focused on character and the most effective medium.

"We decided to use television, so we created our own character Ronald McDonald." *–Ibid*

He was a master of detail and specificity.

"Mr. Turner wrote what was known internally as 'The Bible,' documenting McDonald's pioneering food production. French fries had to be cut exactly

0.28 inches thick. Burgers went on the grill in six neat rows." –*The Wall Street Journal*

And he made sure his audience heard McDonald's story through relentless, jingle-laden TV advertising.

The trouble is that Turner's 20th century application of then-successful traditional storytelling elements—*telling* your audience what you want them to believe and assuming they will—was a strategy that worked until the digital age, when it backfired.

In early 2012, McDonald's went fishing on Twitter for stories about people's positive, wholesome experiences at McDonald's with the hashtag "McDStories." Many of the responses were quite the opposite.

"McDonald's in this case had no idea what their true perception in the marketplace was," said Jason Falls of SocialMediaExplorer.com. "They didn't see their brand the way consumers did. So when they tried to portray their brand as something it wasn't, at least from a perception standpoint, they got dinged."

> And don't forget what happened to poor ol' Robert "call me Bob" McDonald, former top dog at Proctor & Gamble—literally the largest marketer in the known universe—when he dove head first into the shallow end of the social media pool.
>
> One fine January day, Bob announced that P&G would lay off 1,600 marketing employees because, he had come to realize, social media is a tremendously efficient and cost-effective way to communicate with people. That was good news for P&G's bottom line, but it was bad news for Bob, because the January that Bob make that brilliant announcement happened to be in 2012, making him possibly the last person on the planet to learn about the Internet.
>
> Bob "retired" three months later.

And Kodak—the company that made sharing photographs convenient and affordable for everyone—was busy scrambling for bankruptcy protection in January 2012, just weeks before Facebook paid $1 billion for an upstart company called Instagram that made sharing photographs convenient, *free,* and fun for everyone.

It's been a rough ride for the C-suite executive class. But their loss can serve as a lesson to us: if you think you and your organization are immune to the ravages of the disruptive powers of social media, well Neo, it might be time to swallow the red pill.

For those who missed the reference, John is referring to an iconic scene in the movie *The Matrix* when Morpheus offered the protagonist, Neo, two pills. If he chooses the blue pill, he will wake up in his own room and continue to live the fantasy that he once thought was his life. If he chooses the red pill, he will live in actual reality and learn just "how far the rabbit hole goes."

Family Feud: Keeping it real with Sheryl and Mark

Sheryl Sandberg, the chief operating officer at Facebook, best summed up the evolution of the Internet from the "information web" (i.e. Google) to the "social web" (a.k.a. the Interactive Age) with this simple statement: "It's the wisdom of the crowds to the wisdom of friends."

And how will we realize this Internet nirvana? "The social web can't exist until you are your real self online," she said. And she's right.

I have to give credit to both Mark Zuckerberg and Sheryl Sandberg for walking the talk by being their "real selves" when they appeared with Charlie Rose on his self-named talk show.

Throughout the interview, Mark assumed the role of that goofy, whiz-kid billionaire next door, while she played the doting and slightly overprotective momma bear. And I'm pretty sure they weren't acting. The following verbatim exchanges do not do justice to the actual video.

"He's says he remembers caller ID. Next question."

> **Sheryl**: When caller ID was rolled out, and I'm actually old enough to remember this, unlike my friend over here --
> **Mark**: No, I had caller ID.
> **Sheryl**: Do you remember before caller ID?
> **Mark**: Yeah, yeah, yeah.
> **Sheryl**: Oh, that's good. Normally --
> **Charlie Rose**: But you don't remember before caller ID.

That's the point --
Sheryl: No, he says he does.

Charlie: Has the Groupon experience ... changed your sense of timing of an IPO?
Mark: I don't -- I don't think so.
Sheryl: Not really.
Mark: No.
Charlie: When will you decide?
Sheryl: When we're ready.
Mark: Yeah.

Television gold, Jerry! But the truth is Sheryl and Mark are right. We have evolved from being talked to by the Big Three TV networks to talking with our friends in communities all over the Internet. Adjust accordingly.

Closing Bell: The Economics of Information

To understand how things changed so quickly and why it was virtually impossible for the 20th century Masters of the Universe to remain the masters, you have to think of information as a commodity.

For most of human history, the information market was functionally an oligopoly: a few information producers and brokers (royalty, the church, scholarly institutions, *etc.*) dominated the market. Their production systems—chiseled stone, monastically scribed books, a limited run of hand-pressed Bibles—were expensive and labor-intensive. As a result, there was an extremely high "price" for accumulating information, which restricted learning to those who had stature and wealth.

During the Industrial Age, the supply of information gradually broadened as universal education became widespread. During the Information Age, however, the supply of information exploded as technological advancements lowered the price for the production and accumulation of information.

The supply of information greatly outpaced its demand long ago. Anyone who's ever been to a library has seen a vast amount of information languishing on dusty shelves.

Ironically, in the Information Age, information became less valuable than ever before. But because the channels over which this "cheap" information flowed was until recently controlled by corporations, the media, Hollywood, and the recording and publishing industries, the price for that information could be artificially manipulated. As long as they controlled the distribution

"Here are the edits from Legal. And the old man wants it out by the High Middle Ages at the latest."

of information, these multi-billion-dollar industries thrived, generating profits that would make a banker blush.

The Internet broke the lock on the flow of information and people began freely sharing ideas, images, videos, music, and art. Where consumers once paid money to receive information (via subscriptions, cable fees, telephone bills, movie tickets), they are now getting it and *giving it away* for free.

9 **Today, the value of information is not predicated on how much people are willing to pay to receive it. It is determined by how many people want to share it.**

The consistent delivery of relevant, accessible, and/or entertaining content will build "brand loyalty" that can be used to earn revenue the old-fashioned way, while also creating an emotionally invested community of supporters.

Another World: Communications challenges and opportunities in the Interactive Age

In the Interactive Age, you need a lot more than a good product and a catchy jingle to get (and keep) your audience's attention and engage their emotions. However, you can now communicate with them more easily, cheaply, and frequently. And co-creating a community based on your organization's story, when done successfully, yields a multiplier effect far in excess of what you could possibly purchase through traditional advertising. Unless you had Proctor & Gamble's ad budget, of course.

But before you can build this community, you must grab the attention of the people in your audiences, interact with them, and earn and maintain their trust.

> And it ain't easy. At eight seconds, our average attention span is shorter than that of a goldfish. And when we're online, we make that goldfish look like a Russian chess master.

1. *The Young and the Restless:* Dealing with short attention spans

> One of the most frightening horror movie scenes I've ever seen is the single-camera shot of six-year-old Danny Lloyd riding his Big Wheel through the great room, halls, and kitchen of the haunted Overlook Hotel in Stanley Kubrick's *The Shining*. It goes on for over a minute with only one splice of the steadicam footage. During that time absolutely *nothing* happens. And to this day, it scares the bejeesus out of me.
>
> A few years back, when *Ion Television* rebroadcast *The Shining*, I told my daughters to get ready to see one of the most frightening scenes in horror movies. But even before Danny turned the first corner, I looked over to see one of my kids texting and the other on her tablet. The subtle build-up of tension was completely lost on a generation that grew up with split-second video cuts.

So how do you hold the attention of a generation of kids who can barely sit through a six-second Vine video?

There are two main stages that you have to navigate: you must *capture* and then *keep* your audience's attention. Getting their attention requires a concise "teaser" that makes the prospect of engaging more enticing than spending that time texting, watching a movie, playing a game ... or doing all of the above.

My favorite approach is to start a story with "Did I ever tell you about the time ..." a la Gabe *"Welcome Back"* Kotter.

But the trick is, the events have to be true and they should relate to the bigger story you want to tell.

- "Did I ever tell you about the time I found that boa constrictor on 8th Street SE in DC?"
- "Did I ever tell you about the time that cowboy tried to kill me with a Galliano bottle?"
- "Did I ever tell you about the state parliamentarian, the prostitute, and the New York correspondent for *Pravda*?"

And the list goes on.

You can also grab your audience's attention by opening your story with a reference that is significant to them.

"I want this story on every doorstep by tomorrow night! That's right, I said *tomorrow!*"

Like sewer monsters.

What? You know what, forget it. I don't want to know.

Once you have their attention, you need to continue getting it at frequent intervals. There is a constant calculation of "Is this still worth the entertainment I'm giving up right now?"

We all have less time and more options than ever before, and it makes for a mean competitive environment when attempting to communicate.

The Munsters: How your audience's inner monster can give your story legs

Do you fist pump when your toilet flushes properly? Yeah, me neither. Unless you're a drug dealer, a functioning toilet isn't a matter of life or death. You just expect it to work.

And therein lays the problem for municipal sewer authority public information officers (or PIOs).

Nobody cares that the sewage system infrastructure is doing its job. It's when it isn't that the conversation starts. And if the effluence hits the affluent, watch out! It's emergency city council hearings and "the full story at 11" on channel 9.

I learned this in Napa, where I was speaking to the California Association of Public Information Officials. During Q & A, the PIO for a municipal sewer authority asked, "What is the best way to inform our customers that our system has the lowest rate of incidents in the region and that we have never gone over budget?"

"There is no good way. Nobody cares. Much like a dependable toilet, you're doing what people expect you to do."

"But my boss wants me to get the word out and I'm having a very difficult time."

"I'll bet. Let me ask you a question. Have you ever seen the video of the North Carolina sewer monster? Because people care about the North Carolina sewer monster."

The NCSM is a blob of wormy tentacles that actually moves when it senses danger. The video—which showed several of these critters living in the sewers of Raleigh, NC—got over 5 million hits on YouTube and was featured on *ABC World News Tonight*.

"Aligning your organization's story with a popular story or video is a great way to grab people's attention."

Awkward silence, then ...

> "But my boss doesn't want us to show our customers videos of sewer monsters. He wants us to tell them about our incident-free system and sound budget management."
>
> "Let's break it down," I said, drawing two circles on the white board. "The big circle on the left represents everything you could possibly say about the sewer authority. The small circle on the right represents everything your customers want to hear about the sewer authority. You see that tiny spot where the two circles touch? That's sewer monsters. And the best way to get information from your circle into their circle is through that tiny sewer-monster connection."

Moving on …

Anyone who's ever read fiction knows the traditional format: you set the stage and then have a sequence of actions that lead to a resolution of some sort.

The entertainment comes from traversing the journey with the characters in the book, and the ending is the big (or disappointing) payoff for all of that invested time. It's a simple, linear model that our brains have adapted to over millennia. And it still has huge value in communicating information and establishing emotional connections.

But the rise of texting, tweeting, and uber-short video clips—along with the sheer amount of information the average person deals with each day—has driven the development of different learning strategies.

One of the most common approaches can be imagined as a pyramid.

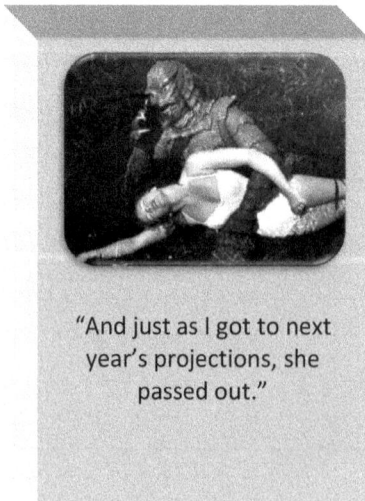

"And just as I got to next year's projections, she passed out."

10 As people are sifting through huge quantities of information, it is the small, catchy "essence" that will cause them to pause.

From there, *if they are interested*, they will spend increasing amounts of time and energy to fill in more of the details and back story that form the bulk behind that one point at the tip of the pyramid.

Rather than the gradual build-up to a climax, the new reality requires that you start with a bang, and seed each level of detail with more value in order to create incentives for the audience to stick with you.

Once again, TV offers a viable communications model. Why do you become interested in a TV show? Probably because of a 30-second clip that compiled the most exciting and intriguing parts of an upcoming episode. The episode is designed to hook you long before the first commercial break. And then at the end of that episode, you get another teaser of an upcoming episode. Tantalize, deliver, repeat. And never bury the lead.

> Megan, did you ever see that *Bones* episode that opened with these guys trying to get a corpse out of a grease trap and when they lifted it up the whole thing …

I did, John. Try to focus …

So ask yourself, "what would your organization's teaser be?"

2. *Different Strokes:* The Death of "the Public"

In the Information Age, we were (generally) able to share a set of cultural norms and experiences to create a (generally) mutual understanding of morality and reality. The Interactive Age signifies the end of any opportunity to "teach the world to sing, in perfect harmony." Instead, the Internet has given everyone the opportunity to apply their own, highly fluid set of beliefs and experiences to their entertainment and information choices, which ultimately determine what information they consume and who they share it with.

These beliefs and experiences bring people together in online tribes—some large, some small. Some long-lasting, some just short bursts of communal energy—but all of which are constantly in flux.

This creates another distinct challenge for organizations trying to tell their story or communicate a consistent brand image: different people will interpret and react to these efforts in different ways and at different times.

For instance, compare the norms of earlier days to those of today. Ads that might have drawn a giggle or a wink in 1963 could cause you physical harm today.

And because there is no "sunset provision" for information in the Interactive Age, you have to be mindful of how your messages today play in the not-too-distant future. You are communicating with a spectrum of generations, beliefs, knowledge bases, *etc.* every time you post online.

11 **One way to facilitate communication among very different communities is to spell out the assumptions and beliefs that are behind any given conclusion.**

With organizational storytelling, this translates into considering your organization as a new world for your audience. Like a TV show, it may have many similarities to the world that some of these individuals inhabit, but interaction is aided by repeatedly citing the core tenets on which your communications are based.

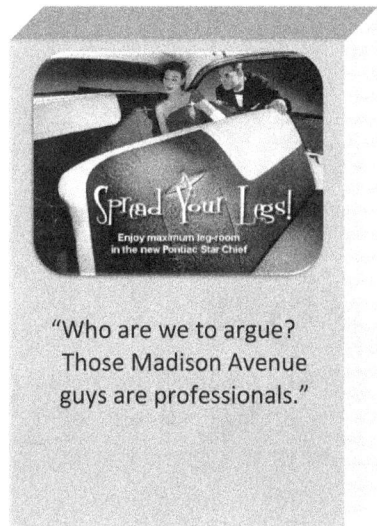

Spread Your Legs!

Enjoy maximum leg-room in the new Pontiac Star Chief

> Let me offer an example, Megan. Did you ever see that Star Trek episode about the *Yangs* and the *Kohms*, these two barbarian tribes that were fighting each other? Well, as it turns out, these tribes actually represented the Yankees and the Communists on some parallel—but very different—planet. So when Kirk convinces the

"Who are we to argue? Those Madison Avenue guys are professionals."

two tribes to work together in peace, he essentially ended the Cold War that clung on to a small part of practically everyone's brain back in the late 1960s.

Well, there you go.

3. *Whose Line Is It Anyway:* Communicating with an Interactive Audience

12 **Your audience is no longer a passive group that enters into your situational construct. They react, interpret, and change it—even as you first produce it and long after you've moved on to other projects.**

TV is adapting to this very challenge. In the early days of television, the only thing you ever heard from the audience was Desi Arnez's distinctive off-screen laugh as he reacted to the filming of *I Love Lucy.* Today, game shows, reality shows, even scripted shows are deliberately interacting with their studio audiences and those playing along at home via websites and social media.

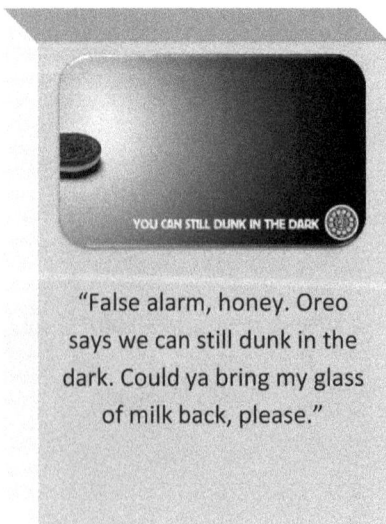

YOU CAN STILL DUNK IN THE DARK

"False alarm, honey. Oreo says we can still dunk in the dark. Could ya bring my glass of milk back, please."

It has gotten so common that in 2013 Nielsen, the TV rating system, and Twitter teamed up to create the Nielsen Twitter TV rating service.

This interactive world offers huge bonuses for organizations that are able to take advantage of developments in real time. For instance, Oreo was able to create a social media sensation by tweeting out this image during the 2013 Super Bowl blackout.

Consider it virtual karma: the more

clever, unique, and admirable things that you and your organization do, the more likely it is that people will notice you doing them.

13 **While there's value in sharing your accomplishments, there's less need (and less benefit) in tooting your own horn than in previous times. You still discuss your activities, of course. You just do so more gracefully and subtly than before.**

But the reverse is also true. People are much more likely to notice the selfish, stupid, and embarrassing things you do, too. Even if it escapes immediate scrutiny, the Internet has no expiration date. You and your organization can be exposed at any time for things you did months, years, and (soon) decades ago.

Even if you sell no-kill critter traps, there will always be someone who opposes your organization and what it stands for. Expect these digital muckrakers to examine, fact-check, and call you on your actions.

Remember, Karma's a bitch and she knows where you get your coffee.

But by dealing honorably and transparently with your audiences and openly admitting and fixing your mistakes, you can build a stronger and more vocal group of supporters than you were previously able to do.

4. *Trust Me:* Earning trust in the Interactive Age

When did "a cup of coffee" become "a tall, double-shot dry latte with two pumps of caramel"?

By any measure, we have more choices than any previous generation. As a result, we make more decisions than ever before in human history.

But the evolutionary desire to preserve our focus by basically limiting our own choices has not changed. And the most crucial filter was (and remains) an issue of trust. If you are going to sub-contract out some of the intellectual computing that goes into decision-making—as the explosion of online information essentially does—who do you trust?

In earlier periods, when change moved more slowly, relying on your elders was a sound decision. If eating those speckled berries didn't kill your forebears, they likely wouldn't kill you either. It wasn't a lack of rationality or free will. It's simply that in a world full of uncertainty and with a limited ability to discern facts, following established paths was an excellent survival mechanism.

But in the Industrial Age, and more dramatically in the Information Age, people were dealing with decisions, situations, and information that their forebears couldn't have imagined. The "wisdom of the ages" became a less reliable guide for decision-making because the ages hadn't confronted these challenges before.

Concurrent with the fall of tradition was the rise of the "expert." Where the "old ways" had lapsed in influence, science and specialization was there to aid decision-making. When four out of five doctors recommended a product, we were confident that buying it was the right thing to do. The "expert" had replaced the "sage."

But with the advent of the Internet, it became possible to fact-check "the establishment" in real time, because the audience now has access to the same information as the experts. You could now theoretically trust in your own research. No relying on "experts."

The only problem is that the explosion of data, multiplicity of interpretations, and sheer time and energy it takes to weed through the ever-expanding font of information meant that uncertainty once again reached a paralyzing threshold.

So if you can't trust tradition, or the experts, or anyone who is potentially influenced by financial motivations, then who do you trust?

You trust yourself, your friends, your online communities. You trust experiences over "facts" or compilations of data when you believe that the latter are regularly manipulated. You trust "Anne from WI" over any given expert, because Anne is theoretically less likely to have her own agenda.

And you turn fiercely on Anne if it turns out that she is actually an employee of a given company, because she has not only lied but misrepresented herself as "one of us." A corporation in consumer's clothing, as it were.

The rise of search, social, and mobile aided this transition—it's incredibly simple to ask your friends for real-time input or to do on-the-spot price comparisons for almost any given item. And while companies in the Information Age largely competed by offering a variety of products or lower prices, in the Interactive Age price is no longer the prime consideration.

14 **Instead of blindly accepting the sales pitches of corporations, people are making purchasing decisions based on their beliefs and experiences with a given company.**

Candid Camera: Live by video, die by video

We weren't very technologically savvy when I was a kid. Tonka trucks were about as high-tech as we got, and that only lasted until we tangled up the black string that operated the claw pulley.

Real technology was reserved for special occasions. A Timex watch was a special birthday present; you got an electric typewriter for graduating from high school; and a new TV console delivered to *anybody's* house triggered a barbeque for the entire neighborhood.

But today, every kid in America is carrying all that and more in a device the size of dog's paw. One significant outcome of these technological advances is that just about everyone now has access to the tools and distribution channels necessary to create and disseminate their own written, audio, and video communications in real time. That's the good news.

The bad news: if you find yourself acting up at the company Christmas party, that video just might star you.

The world is now one huge recording studio, and the spotlight can be turned on you or your organization at any moment. And you may not realize it's happened until you watch it on YouTube.

It's easier than ever for an opponent to ambush anyone in your organization at any time, and share the resulting conversation with the world. For this reason, you need to *live* your organization's story by incorporating the beliefs and philosophies that drive it into your work and personal life.

Doing so will help prepare you for such confrontations, since you will effectively become a personification of your organization's values. And since any of your staff can be put on the spot at any time, it makes sense to invest in their ability to effectively tell your organization's story as well.

"Don't worry, little girl. The Internet hasn't been invented yet. Your secret is safe with us and all the folks watching at home."

Find Your Story

Once Upon a Time: Imagining your organization's most compelling stories

> The future belongs to a very different kind of person with a very different kind of mind—creators and empathizers, pattern recognizers, and meaning makers.
>
> These people—artists, inventors, designers, storytellers, caregivers, consolers, big picture thinkers—will now reap society's richest rewards and share its greatest joys.
>
> *– Daniel Pink*

Every organization has a story to tell.

A story that separates them from their competitors.
A story that commands the attention and support of their constituents.
A story that captures the spirit of their quest, and the unique power of their team.

But too often, these once-vibrant stories are diluted by legal counsel, industry jargon, and mandatory sign-offs from multiple department heads. Over time these engaging stories are typed up into a framed "mission statement" that hangs lifelessly on the workroom wall by the copy machine.

What sets *successful* organizations apart—whether it's a small business, a philanthropic nonprofit, or a large corporation—is that **the work being done has meaning.**

15 **It doesn't matter if you're selling a product, providing a service, or advancing an idea, success today depends on doing work that reflects your values—and conveying those values to your audience through stories.**

To get to the heart of your organization's story, you have to ask yourself: What is my organization trying to accomplish?

It seems like a simple question, but you'd be surprised how many people—

even among an organization's leadership—don't know the answer. The answer to that question, however, is the basis for everything you need to do to tell your story effectively.

Let's talk Oreos again.

Talk what?

Oreos. It's not just a cookie. It's a flash mob. It's a meme. It's a YouTube sensation. It's a Twitter genius. It's a Facebook monster. It's milk's favorite cookie.

It wasn't always this way. Oreos used to be just a snack, like Twinkies, Ring Dings and Devil Dogs. But while Nabisco was celebrating Oreo's 100th birthday with flash mobs and online events, Hostess was filing for bankruptcy protection, which briefly killed off the much-maligned Twinkie at the relatively young age of 82. (The Hostess bankruptcy also put Drakes Cakes out of business, shutting down—at least temporarily—the Ring Ding and Devil Dog assembly line.)

How did Oreos become a global Internet sensation just as Hostess was throwing in the apron? Because Nabisco used social media to tell the story they wanted to tell that would resonate with the audiences they needed to reach. They carefully planned and deftly executed intricate campaigns and skillfully seized unexpected opportunities. And they did it creatively, humorously, and relentlessly.

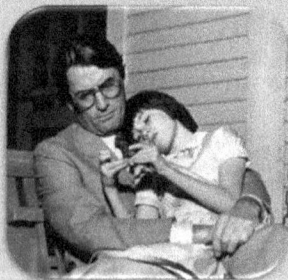

"Why did I prosecute? Well, Scout, some marketing campaigns are so bad they're actually criminal."

It wasn't a story about sweet white stuff slapped between two black wafers. It was a story about *your* experience with their cookie. For Baby Boomers, the story was a nostalgic trip back to childhood. For the Millennials, the story was exciting, edgy and often political. And for the young ones, it was a story about Grandma and imagination.

Hostess, on the other hand, allowed the Twinkie story to be told by others. And we know how well that turned out.

How Tequila Marketing Opportunity

Speaking of Oreos, Megan … what do Oreo cookies and Cuervo Gold have in common?

Can't think of a thing, John.

Exactly. Nothing. And it should probably stay that way. The mere thought of an Oreo-rita makes me … let's just say, uncomfortable. But Team Cuervo Gold can still learn a trick or two from Team Oreo.

During the 2013 Super Bowl (that's the night that the lights went out in Nawlins), Oreo carped the diem by conceiving, creating, approving, and tweeting a graphic ad that capitalized on the Superdome's power struggle—in just five minutes. The ad got re-tweeted thousands of times, and the brilliant marketing move was talked about worldwide. For free.

Cuervo Gold, on the other hand, was MIA on a night they should have owned. Think about it. What does the Spanish word "cuervo" mean? Raven (well, actually "crow," but you get my point). And what were the 49ers panning for? Gold. Correct. Soooo … ?

So you have a Super Bowl that pits the "Cuervos" against the freakin' "Golds"! The possibilities for drink recipes alone are mind-boggling. How about a "Tequila Mockingbird" for the San Francisco Chroniclers? Or "Gold on the Rocks" for the Raven lunatics?

And yet there was not one chirp, not one "Eureka!" from the good folks at Jose Cuervo, Inc. That, my friends, is marketing malpractice.

Don't let your story be trumped by a cookie. Learn from Cuervo's gaffe and Oreos' staff. According to *The Washington Post,* Oreo's ad team "required that ad agency and client executives be at the same place at the same time" which was a "social-media command center" at its digital ad agency 360i in NYC.

That is the reality of storytelling today. You've got to be quick. You've got to be relevant. And you have got to execute. The days of "running it by legal" are over.

"That never woulda happened on my watch."

Does *your* team know your organization's story? Try this little experiment: ask your staff to name their favorite TV show and describe what it's about in 10 seconds. Now ask them describe what your organization is about in 10 seconds. Chances are, people found it easier to describe their favorite TV show than the work they do.

And that's a problem. Here's the solution.

Step 1: Find your organization's quest

Your organization's quest is the pursuit of that goal that gets you—and all successful people—out of bed in the morning and keeps driving you to give your all, even when you are overworked and underpaid. And it is this quest that is at the heart of your story.

Consider the following hypothetical elevator speeches about Jump$tart, an organization that … well, I'll let them tell you.

Elevator Speech #1: Recite your mission statement

"So what do you do?"

"I'm with Jump$tart, a national coalition of organizations dedicated to improving the financial literacy of pre-kindergarten through college-age youth by providing advocacy, research, standards and educational resources. Jump$tart strives to prepare youth for life-long successful financial decision-making."

Likely reply: "Uhh … this is my floor. Have a good one!"

Elevator Speech #2: Share your quest

"So what do you do?"

"I'm with Jump$tart. We teach kids about money."

Even more likely reply: "Really? I wish I knew how you do that because my kids know bupkis about managing money. Do you have a card?"

Conversation initiated.

16 **When you connect with your core audience and share with them the passion you have for the work your organization does, you will inspire them to join you in your quest.**

But you have to act fast. Your window of opportunity to share your quest with someone new is rarely open wide enough to shove your mission statement through.

So, what is your organization's passion? How are *you* trying to better the world?

Here are three simple questions to ask yourself and your leadership team as you seek to identify your organization's quest.

- **What is the one way your product or service can benefit society?** Harley Davidson sells freedom. AAA offers peace of mind. Hell, even Oreo has a quest. So while your mission may be to sell milkshakes or membership, your quest should be how people will benefit from those milkshakes and increased membership.

- **Who or what *exactly* will benefit from your product or services?** Remember, you don't have to save the world. You may find that your organization is a tremendous asset to a very narrow segment of society or just a tiny bit of our environment. *The American Dehydrated Onion and Garlic Association** may not swing a big bat in DC but you can be damned sure that the nation's onion and garlic dehydrators value their contribution in defense of their proud industry. (*Yup. You can look it up.)

- **Is your quest realistic and achievable?** The Leukemia and Lymphoma Society ran an ambitious marketing campaign that asked people to pledge that "cancer ends with me." This is a worthy goal, to be sure. But the LLS is setting themselves up for failure. Once you've secured a pledge you have solidified your bond with your target audience. As generous and as patient as they may be, they will one day want their pledge fulfilled … by you.

Benefits of a quest-oriented organization

Your quest is more than just the heart of your organization's story. Here are just a few ways your quest helps your organization achieve its mission:

- **A quest provides definition.** A quest helps to encapsulate both what your organization does and, more importantly, *why* it does it.

- **Quests provide a shared lens for engagement.** Whether it's internally or externally, a quest helps frame discussions, explain setbacks, and provide a collective way to experience the world.

- **Quests are an avenue of persuasion.** A quest that others can agree with provides common ground and a starting point for discussion, making it easier to build bridges, negotiate, or persuade.

- **Quests drive intentional change.** Your quest should function as a "North Star" to help navigate daily decisions as well as shape larger strategies and goals.

With this perspective, a group's quest is not the province of PR, marketing, sales, or advertising folks. It is everyone's job to maintain, improve, and otherwise contribute to the success of the quest, since that story is the symbolic "life's blood" of the organization.

The stonecutter's parable

A man walked up to a stonecutter and asked what he's doing. The stonecutter replied, "I'm busting up these damn rocks. What does it look like I'm doing?"

When the man asked another stonecutter the same question, the man looked up, smiled, and said, "I'm helping to build a beautiful cathedral."

And then the foreman showed up, tossed the guy off the work site and docked each stonecutter a day's pay for goofing off.

Not helpful, John.

Duck Dynasty: How a bunch of duck hunters swept the environmentalists off their feet

Another benefit of identifying your organization's quest is that you overtly develop common ground with other organizations. Take Ducks Unlimited, for example. There are relatively few organizations that are going to publicly advocate for the right to blow birds out

"I found my Quest and my Hadji, but where's my Bandit?"

of the sky.

But a number of different groups— from environmental activists to bird-watching societies—would find the quest to preserve wetlands and waterfowl appealing and a natural fit with their organization.

Ducks Unlimited has a quest that truly inspires people to act. The sportsmen's group boasts of being "the world's leader in wetlands and waterfowl conservation," which is true. And, as a result, "Ducks Unlimited does more than any other organization to put ducks in the sky," which is also true. And they then shoot more ducks *out* of the sky than any other organization.

You could say that making sure there are ducks to kill today and in the future is their true goal—their mission, if you will—given that about 90 percent of their members are hunters. But they (wisely) keep the focus on their quest (which happens to further their goal).

Compare that to the American Dairy Association. Their mission is "to economically benefit dairy farmers by encouraging the consumption of milk and dairy products through advertising, education and promotion, to reach consumers with product benefits and advantages."

A worthy endeavor if you're a dairy farmer. But the quest of "economically benefitting dairy farmers" is not likely to convince people to buy more milk. So while the ADA is being candid about their perfectly legitimate mission, they are missing the opportunity to connect with their audience, who might otherwise be persuaded to offer assistance.

"I just thought you should know before you wrote them anonther check."

And they are not alone. Take a gander at your own mission statement. Go ahead; we'll wait. So is your mission about helping other people?

Step 2: Identify your audience

In story development, there's a hot dispute between whether a story should be plot-driven or character-driven. And in organizational storytelling, many recommend that your "customer" (however you define it in each case) be the hero of your story.

While these drivers are appropriate for certain types of stories, **in the Interactive Age, your *story* is what your quest means to your audience.**

And since your quest is an internalized journey that your organization is embarking upon, it should not be audience-driven. Your quest dictates the audience you will attract, not the reverse.

17 | **The *story* is neither solely about your quest nor your audience, but rather how your audience perceives and interacts with your quest.**

Think of the whole quest-audience-story relationship as a journey. Your **quest** is your destination, your **audiences** are the people you meet along the way, and your **story** is the conversation you have with these folks.

Here's a *ferinstance*. I once ran the American Beverage Institute, a restaurant trade association dedicated to protecting the rights of adults to drink responsibly prior to driving—or as one reporter crudely put it, I "defended drinking and driving for a living." While technically accurate, I saw our **quest** as protecting responsible adults from the wrath of anti-alcohol evangelists while encouraging law enforcement to focus on the real drunk driving problem—alcohol abusers and other ne'er-do-wells.

During our journey, we met a lot of people who held quite diverse opinions on this issue. To our supporters, we told cautionary tales that highlighted why they should join us in our quest, not the least of which being self-preservation. To the media and lawmakers, we told fact-based stories about the real source of the drunk driving problem, with recommendations from numerous law enforcement officials on how best to get these drunks off the road.

To our detractors ... well, there wasn't a lot of storytelling. But there was the occasional shouting match, which really didn't help anybody.

Breaking Bad:
Three lessons that will help you tell the hard truths

I know what you're thinking. Did he really just say that he defended drinking and driving for a living? Well, to tell you the truth, in all the excitement I used to ask that question a lot myself. But seeing that the drunk-driving arrest limit is .08% BAC and that a 120-lb. woman can be arrested for drunk driving if she drinks two glasses of wine over a two-hour period, you've got to ask yourself one question: have you ever had a drink before driving? Well, have you … punk?

I hardly ever went full Clint Eastwood when defending the legality of drinking a beer at a ballgame. But I did bring up the 120-lb. woman … *ad nauseum*. Because it is indeed a US DOT-certified fact that this proverbial 120-lb. woman who drank two six-ounce glasses of wine over a two-hour period would exceed the drunk driving arrest threshold. But it is also a fact that a 170-lb. man could drink more than four beers in the same timeframe before he blew his way into a jail cell. And "more than four beers" sounds a lot worse than "a couple of glasses of wine."

Now, I'm sure you're wondering, "Why did he bring this up now? We were just starting to get along, and now ... this." Four reasons. Well, one reason and three lessons.

The reason: I want to show you how to deal with controversial issues so you can become a better communicator.

The lessons:

When conveying controversial, data-heavy information, wrap it in a vignette that people can relate to. People can see a 120-lb. woman having two glasses of wine at a restaurant, and the image doesn't comport with their reflexive notion of a drunk driver. Mental dissonance like this often forces people to open the hood and have a quick look at their preconceived notions. Once they do, you've got yourself a conversation.

Tell and retell that vignette. You cannot overshare good information. But you have to try.

Passionately defend what you believe in. Or change jobs. For every organization with a quest, there is another organization opposed to it. And unless you're shilling for deviants like NAMBLA (look it up), you have an obligation to develop compelling stories and convey them in the most creative ways you can to try to achieve your organization's goals. If you're just not that into it, find another job … like I did.

TV shows are a business, with the goal of attracting, recruiting, and retaining an audience—a goal shared by all storytellers, nonprofit and corporate alike.

And while you have many different potential audiences, there is always at least one key group that your quest will naturally resonate with. Start here, with the understanding that your audience is highly fluid—you'll have a semi-permanent core audience, but also temporary participants made up of curious bystanders, your opponents, and those drawn in by external events. Keeping your finger on the pulse of who you're communicating with is one of the major challenges of the Interactive Age.

So who's your key audience?

A. The public
B. Elected officials
C. The media
D. "Influencers"

If you picked any of the above, you've got a problem. Having a focus this broad requires material that is so vanilla as to be useless. So be specific; really, really specific. If your organization were a TV show, would it be targeting the *SNL* crowd or *Barney* aficionados?

Here are some questions that will help you identify your potential audiences:

- What demographic, socio-economic, geographic, and ideological traits make up your key audience?
- Who is financially invested in your quest?
- Who is ideologically aligned/opposed to it?
- Who would benefit if you "won"? "Lost"?
- What platforms do your audiences favor?
- How do they spend their free time?
- Where do their pain points and yours overlap?

Another benefit to having a well-defined and micro-targeted audience is that it makes trust-building a bit easier. Because the fact is, no one is inclined to trust you until you've earned that trust.

Starting with a group that has a natural affinity or interest in your organization's quests allows you to begin adding value to the conversations and debates that are already going on. And it will take a while. Unlike speaking with people in a bar or at church or school, there is very little context online. As a result, connecting requires more "data points" of good information, helpful comments, and entertaining anecdotes to create a trustworthy reputation in your audience's mind.

And much like a TV show, your organization must display consistency even as the world changes around you. That doesn't mean that you can't adjust your storyline as circumstance warrant. You can and you will. But it does mean that you have to keep these adjustments in line with your quest.

Think about the variables you control, and what you can offer that is attractive to a given audience *now*. Then get creative about how your quest can be reimagined or better explained to attract some unconventional audiences.

This Old House:
Building a relationship one tweet at a time

The International Wood Products Association represents companies that import wood from around the world. Their number-one legislative goal is to fix a glaring unintentional flaw the *Lacey Act*—a law designed to prevent the illegal importation of plants, animals, and wood.

This is not really a chart-topper on the *List of Things the Public Generally Cares About,* but Brent McClendon—who ran the association and was as passionate about imported wood as a rational person could be—devised a clever communications strategy that attracted the attention of some interesting people who have probably never heard of the IWPA. With a Twitter-heavy outreach strategy, Brent let his followers know the true nature of Lacey's flaws, including the fact that under the Lacey Act, cellist Yo Yo Ma could be unintentionally breaking the law every time he travels with his 18th century cellos.

Because Brent methodically posted interesting tweets, this and other outlandish realities found their way to Bob Vila's twitter account, prompting the legendary home-improvement guru to start following IWPA. To put this in perspective, at the time, Vila had over *one million followers*, while he followed only several hundred people.

Step 3: Find your conflict

Name a TV show without a conflict. Can't think of one? Exactly.

It's not a coincidence that TV shows are overtly developed around a conflict. Whether it's competing to win $1 million, solving a murder, or trying to get off a creepy island, the "will they or won't they" question hooks people, creating an emotional connection not only with the characters but also with your judgment about what you think will happen.

And that engagement creates the opportunity for the TV producers to expose new information, reposition existing knowledge, and thereby change people's minds—about the characters, the show, the desired outcome, and more.

The word "conflict" comes from the Latin *conflictus,* which can be loosely translated as "colliding" or "combatting." Conflict is about the meeting of two different "forces"—these can be ideas, people, societies, offers, you name it. Conflict is really an umbrella term that includes competitions of all kinds—whether it's two teams meeting on a playing field, two companies competing for market share, or individuals competing to get a promotion at a company.

18 | **Conflict is an essential part of every story. A story without conflict is propaganda.**

Another facet of conflict that is often overlooked is its vital role in mental and emotional activity. Just as teams might scrimmage, ideas and emotions are constantly battling for dominance within individuals, groups, and societies.

It's easy to identify the conflict behind dissenting opinions or protests, but it also plays a key role in teaching. Every time a person learns something, a battle has occurred between the new idea and what previously occupied its place.

This is one of the reasons why debunking misinformation can be a powerful way to persuade: it devalues the existing or competing idea while elevating its replacement.

Moreover, conflict is the key to creating change. Any aspiration—whether it's a hope, a prayer, a quest, or a wish on a star—represents a point of conflict: where "what is" and "what might be" meet. And when they meet on a more concrete plane, you can expect some people to support one side or the other. But without this meeting and contest, change would be impossible.

Every organization has at least one problem that it's trying to solve, whether it's ending world hunger or building a better mousetrap. But this paradigm is inherently static: here's the problem, and here's how our solution will fix it. Instead, recast it as a struggle between the forces that cause or support the problem and the efforts to provide a solution. Now it's a dynamic conflict, allowing for setbacks, twists, and evolution.

Conflict is the natural byproduct of forming an opinion.

Our ability to make judgments about the world around us—the utility, morality, and attractiveness of ideas, events, and people that we come into contact with—is not just a key survival skill. It's also the key to driving engagement and effecting change.

After making a judgment, most people become emotionally attached to it. This is both the good news and the bad news.

On the one hand, it takes a lot of effort to get people to change their minds (and it's not always possible). On the other hand, that emotional investment in their opinion means that they are emotionally invested in the issue about which the judgment was formed—they are *interested* in the debate and have a psychic reward for engaging. And without engagement (or conflict, if you will), there can be no change.

Don't let a good conflict go to waste.

The flip side of being judgmental is the natural human desire to be liked. Again, it's a survival trait—and just as with making judgments, it's extremely hard to disable or suppress.

Anyone who's kept quiet while observing obviously incorrect diatribes on Facebook, at a cocktail party, or around the office has experienced the desire for peace and likeability winning a conflict with their judgment.

But it's also an opportunity missed. Because conflict is *engagement*. It's a chance to trade ideas, communicate, and hopefully teach others something that they didn't know. And maybe even learn something yourself.

If you approach it in this light, you will be better able to align your judgments and your desire to be liked: you are not trying to antagonize anyone, you want to engage with them—learn why they think what they think, share why you think what you do, and see if you can find some common ground.

Anger makes your stories more memorable.

According to *Psychology Today*, "People ruminate about events that induce strong negative emotions five times as long as they do about events that induce strong positive ones."

A Case Western University paper, cryptically entitled "Bad Is Stronger than Good," declared, "The greater power of bad events over good ones is found in everyday events ... Bad emotions, bad parents, and bad feedback have more impact than good ones, and bad information is processed more thoroughly than good."

There's a reason for this, of course. These negative emotions—fear, anger, sadness, envy—generally require some sort of action on our part to shed them. In countless cases, negative emotions (fear foremost among them) have helped our species survive.

So if you want to tell a memorable story, you're going to have to mess with people's chi. Just don't be a jerk about it.

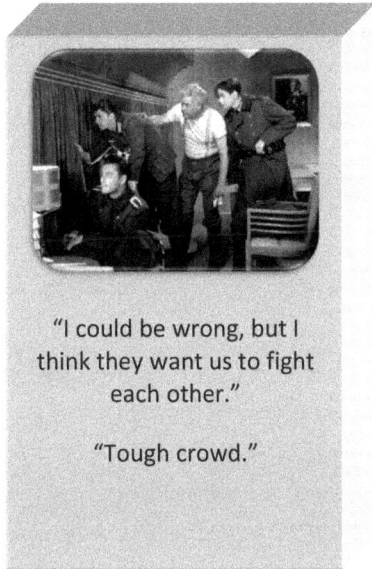

"I could be wrong, but I think they want us to fight each other."

"Tough crowd."

In fact, your civility should increase proportionately with the intensity of the fight. Nobody likes a sore winner or a whiney loser. So do try to maintain a certain approach towards conflict—be respectful, civil, and empathetic.

And if you do find your engine revving in the red zone, here is a line that encompasses respect, civility, and empathy: "That's a fascinating point. And I'd love to agree with you, but then we'd both be wrong."

Remember:

- **Everybody has a story**
- **Every story has a conflict**
- **Every conflict is an opportunity**

Step 4: Set the tone

When you sit down to watch your favorite TV show, you know you're in for a little romance, comedy, mystery, gun play, staged reality, and/or science fiction. You know this because your show's producers have worked hard to create a world of romance, comedy, mystery, gun play, staged reality, or science fiction that you have come to rely on.

The tone of the show is more than the sum of its parts—the setting, the dialogue, the costumes, and the characters. The same should be true with your organization.

The tone is the embodiment and distillation of your organization's frame of reference, its relationship with the world. And it is part of what helps create a common language and understanding that allows you, your staff, and your supporters to easily explain, advocate, and communicate on behalf of your organization.

Strangeness on a Train

The tone is also the language you employ to convey mood and emotion. Whether light-hearted, patriotic, somber, or silly, it's important to employ the appropriate words and imagery that convey that tone. For example, there's nothing funny about people jumping in front of trains to end their tormented lives ... usually. So when you play suicide for laughs, you should employ a somber tone. We opted for *film noir* for this true story ...

Megan and I were on the 7 a.m. Acela bound for New York when the engineer stomped on the brakes like they owed him money. We were miles from the next station ... and just inches away from caboose-ing the 6:30 a.m. Northeast Regional.

From my window, I could see dozens of commuters stepping off the train, sporting hand-tailored Zegnas and thousand-mile stares. I had to chuckle as these *apprentices of the universe* shuffled toward us, squinting like mole people in the bright sunlight. It looked like career day at Zombie U.

Minutes later, the dazed passengers from that train—there were over 100 of them—crammed into ours. We were packed tighter than a Japanese subway car, but our new guests stayed mum.

Then this short gal with a blond pageboy starts sobbing hysterically about some mooch who mistimed his suicide leap. He got the job done but left a grisly vista for those seated on the left.

With the seal busted, some know-it-all started gabbing about the "protocol for such situations," which included yellow-vested conductors barking through bull horns, a neatly choreographed "disembarkation" routine, and oddly enough, the distribution of free snack packs. The things you learn on the way to the Big City.

On the Acela back to DC that evening, we met a surprising number of people who had started their day on the *Kevorkian Express*. A productive day in the city and a few cold ones had knocked the zombie out of them and loosened their jaw bolts. They were dishing the gruesome details of the morning's entertainment, and we were lapping it up with ladles.

But just as they were getting to the good part, there was a crash that would have startled Buddy Rich and the train made an unscheduled jump on the tracks. Rather than die down, the crash got louder as it rumbled from the cow-catcher to the middle of the car behind us.

I was hoping that the crackling thunder below us was a mangled Pathmark shopping cart, but the veterans among us knew better—another Choo Choo Charlie had taken the A Train to the Promised Land.

As the train came to a stop, everyone froze. It was as quiet as a speakeasy just before the doors get kicked in. Then, before the conductor could grab his bull horn, two of the Ghost Train frequent flyers looked at each other and shouted, "Free Snack Packs!!"

And they were right. The things you learn …

Get Set

Have you ever wondered why many TV shows include repeated background footage of wherever the show is supposed to take place?

Locations are powerful contextual symbols, connoting certain traits or characteristics.

19 **With about 65 percent of the population being visual learners, "location shots" are an effective form of shorthand for communicating themes and reminding viewers of underlying beliefs and assumptions woven into the show.**

Consider the following: What if *Twin Peaks* were set in Boston? It would have been an entirely different show. What if *Friends* or *Seinfeld* were set in a rural community? Again, the shows either would have had to be dramatically changed, or they would be so jolting as to be nonsensical. Phoebe singing "Smelly Cat" on a tractor would play quite differently.

So taking the time to identify the "spiritual home" of your organization is a key part of setting the tone for your story.

Pick a "location" for your organization

Regardless of where it's actually located, chances are that your organization has a culture or "feel" that it tries to communicate. Is it a representation of small-town America in a big city? Is your organization's "cultural home" New York City? Prague? Main Street, USA?

Much to everyone's surprise, *Ghost Hunters in the Lincoln White House* was a dismal failure and was not renewed.

The easiest ways to convey location are through photos, fonts, flavors, and features.

Photos are a no-brainer. Are you an environmental organization based in pavement-covered San Francisco and Washington DC, like the Sierra Club is? Then you, my friend, need high-res photos of the great outdoors— glaciers, mountains, and a bear cub leaning on a redwoods—just as the Sierra Club has.

Fonts are a bit trickier. Unless you're the World Clown Association (which naturally gravitates to fun fonts like **Broadway** and $Jokerman$), you're going to have to give this some thought. Generally speaking, your san serif fonts—the ones with smooth edges like the **Ariel** I write with— convey a more casual feel. While serif fonts such as $Garamond$, which Megan prefers, add a little formality to your text.

"Flavors" are colors, but I couldn't think of a word that meant color that starts with "F." You can get really creative with color. The National Confectioners' Association plays with bright candy-colored, uh, colors that pop off the website. While NORML (the National Association for the Reform of Marijuana Laws) tends toward a soft green—presumably to convey the harmless natural quality of marijuana, while simultaneously preventing adverse reactions from some of their more dedicated followers when they choose to log on.

Features are the favorite Christmas ornaments that you hang up last. Many organizations feature videos of the folks back home who comprise their membership or who consume their products. In fact, online video accounts for 50 percent of all mobile traffic and it will represent 55 percent of all Internet traffic in a few short years, according to Bytemobile Mobile Analytics Report and Cisco. Video is ideal for conveying location (as long as the videos are shot 'on location').

Seven things you can do today
to improve your story

1. Strip down to your BVDs. To everybody but your mother, your organization is just another unknown guitar player on the Venice Beach boardwalk—a Robert John Burck, if you will.

Burck was a "piss-poor, no-good" guitar-playing model who couldn't busk enough change on a good day to buy a venti Frappuccino–until he got naked. Now, Burck (AKA The Naked Cowboy) is a fixture in Times Square who has made a fortune with his trademarked Naked Cowboy franchise. Lesson: Find that one feature that separates you from the pack, and ride it 'til you shred the tires.

2. Hunt down and kill clichés. The cliché is a cunning quarry. It blends in with your creative copy, waiting silently for your reader to stumble upon it and then BAM! It bores them to tears. So be …

Dear God! Nobody move. There's a cliché right above us. Don't panic. Just reach deep into your brain and pull out some creativity. No, the right side, you fool! Dig deeper! I know it's in there. Good. Now, let's pray to God this works.

… It blends in with your creative copy, waiting silently for your reader to stumble upon it and then BAM! It leaps straight into her brain, devouring any interest she may have had in reading further. So be vigilant. The story you save may be your own.

3. Help people *feel* big numbers. Employing the "to-the-moon-and-back" gimmick to explain a big number is like using Ken and Barbie dolls to demonstrate a passionate kiss. If you must drop a big number into your copy, drop it on the audience's feet. Need to show them a trillion? Start with something they can grasp, like a second. *If one million seconds equals 11-and-a-half days, how long is a billion seconds? 32 years. Which means a trillion seconds is 32,000 years.* Brain cramp, right? That's how you leave a mark with a number.

4. Sing your story. A well-written story is a song. Whether it flows lyrically or marches forward with a staccato beat, a good story has a tempo that augments the message and enhances the reader's experience. And it's surprisingly easy to do. As you edit, read your copy out loud. If you don't notice a natural cadence to the narration, try culling a few syllables—through word choice or word chopping—to make your copy more melodic.

5. Don't forget to floss your copy. Even the best copy can get gummed up with jargon, acronyms, and legalese. To prevent unsightly copy-stain buildup, scour your copy vigorously. And be extra vigilant with the phrase "wide variety." If you ever find it in your copy, hit "ctrl A" then "ctrl x." That should clear up the problem right away.

6. Hit on one member of your audience. You wouldn't try to hook up with every person at *Tootsie's Orchid Lounge*, would you? Of course not. You want to focus all that charisma into a single charm-laser to reduce your chance of going home alone. Same with writing. Envision who you are writing for in detail, and then hit that person with all the Cyrano you can muster.

7. Imagine that your new friend has to go to the bathroom. Really bad. Nobody ever complained about a speech being too short. The same goes for just about everything you write. If you spend as much energy compressing your word count as you do finding fun phrases, you will have a more appreciative—and less squirmy—audience.

Pulling it all together

As this point, you should have a decent grasp on what you're trying to achieve, who you're talking to, what obstacles are in the way, and the tone you want to use to communicate.

But just in case you skipped around, here are some of the key points to consider when finding your organization's story:

Key points

- In the Interactive Age, the work performed in successful organizations has meaning.
- To pinpoint that meaning, identify your organization's quest—how it strives to create or prevent change.
- Your story is what your quest means to your audience. So it pays to monitor who they are, what they believe, and how they are changing.
- Having a quest means having a conflict. But it doesn't mean you have to pick a fight.
- Don't let a good conflict go to waste—turn it into a conversation.
- You need to determine the tone of your show and stick to it.

Tell your story

The X Factor: Captivating Your Audience

> The great charm of conversation consists less in the display of one's own wit and intelligence, than in the power to draw forth the resources of others.
>
> —*Jean de La Bruyere*

Good content is necessary but not sufficient for creating a good story. Social media demands personality, charm, creativity, and wit. You *must* tell your story in an engaging way.

Sure, you can continue to "tell" your story—by writing a blog, posting comments on social media platforms, engaging in online conversations, posting or reposting family photos and videos of cats.

But very soon you will not be able to effectively tell your story simply through blog posts and other people's videos. Your audience is going to need to see and interact directly with you and your team via video clips, webinars, Skype conferences, and in person.

Two reasons. First, video gets people's attention. A recent study by an e-tailing group found that 60 percent of online customers will watch videos when they come across them. And with more organizations posting podcasts and hosting live video events, your competition for eyeballs increases every day.

Second, that's where your audience is. With the explosive growth of smart phones and tablets, more people are watching and engaging with video than ever before. And the trend is accelerating.

"Wow, he wasn't kidding. He stinks somethin' awful!"

There was a day when you could stay out of the limelight for fear of "making waves" ... "upsetting your board" ... or "drawing unwanted attention" to your issues. And if you did need to communicate with a particular audience to achieve a particular objective, you could hire a PR firm to help tell that particular story for you.

But those days are over. Your story is being told right now. By others. And you can be pretty sure that they're not telling it the way you would.

Life was simpler before technology kept us all connected 24/7. When you wanted to say something back then, you bought an ad or held a news conference. If you wanted to bury some bad news, you released it late on Friday afternoon. Heck, even the TV channels went to bed after belting out *The Star Spangled Banner* (which always struck me as an odd choice for a lullaby).

But today TV never sleeps. And neither does the Internet. People are signing on to tell your story and tuning in to hear it. If you aren't engaging in the conversation, you're pretty much handing your "channel" over to anyone with Wi-Fi and an agenda.

20   Webinars, Skype, Vine, and other video platforms demand human involvement.

To effectively share your story, you must first understand the customs and mechanics of communicating in the Interactive Age.

You've got to learn how to build a story that will grab your audience by the lapels and shout, "Click me! Like me! Share me!"

You need to master the telling of your story through social media, video, and in person. And you need at least a rudimentary understanding of the differences between various social media platforms to avoid embarrassing situations.

Just as in "real life," the venues you use to communicate have a big effect what you say and how you say it. (That googly-eyed baby talk that entertains your girlfriend will get you tazed if you used it with a cop.)

To understand the new world, consider these old-world examples:

VENUE: Your favorite noisy pub
APPROACH: Loud, off-color comments that you practically spit in your friend's ear.

VENUE: Sunday Mass
APPROACH: Fidgety whispering about how bored you are, accompanied

by crude illustrations drawn with those bowling-alley pencils on the back of the church bulletin.

VENUE: Elevator
APPROACH: Vapid comments about the weather directed to the top of your shoes.

VENUE: Men's room
APPROACH: There is no approach. The first rule of "Men's Room" is you DO NOT talk in the men's room.

The same rules hold true with social media venues. You wouldn't post a video of the shark-cat riding a Roomba on LinkedIn, would you? Of course not. Different venues require different approaches.

The clever folks at MyCleverAgency.com have a creative and suitable-for-framing poster which offers great advice about how to behave on various social media platforms.

For example, they point out that you should keep a positive tone on Facebook, use Twitter for calls to action, and don't post pictures on Pinterest that have human faces.

Good stuff. It's worth a look. (The URL to the chart is incredibly long. Just Google "My Clever Agency" and infographic.)

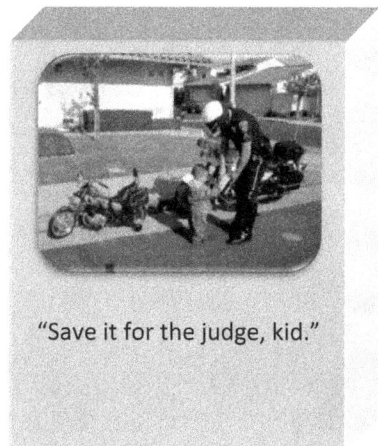

"Save it for the judge, kid."

It's About Time: Mastering the mores and mechanics of storytelling in the Interactive Age

You risk more than embarrassment if you don't abide by the rules and mores of various social media platforms. You risk having your message fall on deaf ears, or worse, trigger a negative reaction—as many gargantuan 20th century institutions have discovered.

History's highway is littered with the wreckage of blue chippers who ignored the "paradigm shift ahead" signs posted by game-changing technologies.

The dead and dying include the Fourth Estate, the film and recording industries, realtors, travel agencies, book publishers, book sellers, bookmakers, brick and mortar retail, and even the porn industry.

Here are just a few doozies:

Twitter Twaddle: Even before Rep. Anthony Weiner cratered his career with inappropriate twitillation, designer Kenneth Cole tested Twitter's boundaries with an astoundingly tone-deaf tweet linking the 2011 Arab Spring and his new Spring line. He failed the test.

Duick T-Bones Toyota: Hoping to generate buzz for Toyota's Matrix, Saatchi & Saatchi LA created an online "stalking" promotion that petrified an unwitting "participant" named Amanda Duick. She sued Toyota for $10 million.

"Complain? Who the hell would complain? It's just a cigarette."

RedFacebook: Threatened by Google's growth, Facebook hired Burson-Marsteller to gin up negative stories about their rival. Being hip, Burson asked an influential blogger to write a Google-bashing op-ed that they would be "happy to place." Being clueless, they refused to tell the blogger who their client was. Imagine Burson's surprise when the blogger passed on writing the op-ed and posted their entire email exchange instead.

But, of course, things could get a lot worse. And often do. (Check out how Xcel energy got out-communicated by a band of activists armed with nothing but the

Internet and a great story in the "Live Your Story" section.)

To see if things could get worse for you, take this simple quiz:

Do you include any of the following among the "critical contributions" you make to your organization?

1. Serving as a conduit between the C-suite and PRNewswire;

2. Making sure that Legal has approved the draft release that's scheduled to go out next Tuesday; or

3. Sitting on the PR Selection Committee to determine which agency your organization will hire to tamp down that ugly flare-up with the Digby account.

If you answered "yes" to any of the above, you need to listen carefully to this eulogy for a travel agent. And then make the appropriate hard choices.

Bones:
Things to do on the Internet when you're already dead

"Let me tell you about Bob. Bob wasn't just my travel agent; he was my friend. Not the come-over-and-watch-the-game-tonight kind of friend. But the kind of friend you'd call when you needed to make travel arrangements. Bob was my go-to guy.

"But Bob saw the writing on the wall. One day when he was booking my trip to Peoria for the Mystery Shopping Providers Association Summit and Expo, he leaned over his desk, and he says to me, he says, 'I can see the writing on the wall. This Internet thing is going to put me out of business.'

"So I say, 'What do you mean, Bob?' And he says, 'Why would anyone hire me—or any travel agent for that matter—to do what they can easily do for themselves online?'

"I said, 'No, Bob! Even if we can book our own travel, we'll always need travel agents because … well because …'

"At that moment, we both knew it was over for him and the travel agent business.

"Bob's with us here today. I can feel his presence. And I can see him right there in the back row. In fact, I see Bob all over town since he got laid off. Poor guy's got nothing to do and all the time in the world to do it. Ain't that right, Bob?"

"Damn straight!"

"So if we learn just one thing from Bob's experience, let it be this: Don't wait for the Internet to put you out of a job. When you see the writing on the wall, teach yourself ways to write better, run faster, and jump higher. Because that's what Bob would have wanted."

"Amen!"

"Thanks, Bob."

"Yes, we've offshored your accounting job, but we've got a special assignment for you in the galley."

Truth or Consequences: The Psychology of Credibility

Because storytelling in the Interactive Age is about sharing and interacting—not just telling—it is essential to build a bond of trust with your audience. And that bond is built on credibility.

Humans are wired to conserve energy and avoid negative experiences. This has two major implications for how you share your story.

The first is based on the concept of "cognitive fluency," which is a fancy way of saying "how easy something is to think about." It's the pretty intuitive idea that people like things that are easy to think about more than those that are hard. And psychologists have found that people's thinking and decision-making is guided by "easy = true" far more than most of us would like. So the easier an idea is to process, the more likely someone is to believe that it's true.

21 **Simplifying your language, making it more enjoyable through rhyming or alliteration, and communicating clearly all help to make your story more credible.**

The second takeaway is related to the first. Since we like things that are easy to process, we tend to like (and trust) familiar things more than new ones. It's part of how public relations and advertising works: you are more likely to think that a statement is true or credible if you've been exposed to it before. Psychologists call this the "illusion of truth," and it's startlingly powerful. A 1992 study from McMaster University in Ontario even found that people will often rate a familiar but false statement as "truer" than a new statement that they know to be true.

These findings make a persuasive case for consistency in persona and message when you are telling your story.

Luckily for independent thinkers everywhere, there's an important loophole to both of these strategies: their effects work best on people who aren't paying much attention or who aren't particularly motivated to find the truth. Once people start concentrating, the weakness or strength of an argument becomes more relevant.

So before you go off thinking that repeating a statement will make it true, remember that in the Interactive Age there's always someone who is paying attention and who is motivated to uncover the truth about what you're saying.

22 **If you lie, you *will* be caught. And once you're caught, expect not only an immediate negative backlash but also a long-term reduction in credibility.**

Inaction speaks louder than words

And if you stay mum hoping your problems will disappear, you're only making things worse. The Internet abhors a vacuum. If you don't tell your stories—the good *and* the bad—others will.

Consider the deafening silence that came from the US Embassy in Nairobi in 2013 after one of their diplomats killed a father of three in a car accident in Kenya. After whisking him back to the States, the Embassy stayed mum about the whole affair. The Internet community, however, filled that vacuum with wall-to-wall vitriol.

"And for God's sake, keep your vacuum away from the Internet. You know how much it hates that thing."

Things only got worse when—nearly a month after the accident—US embassy officials in Nairobi sent the man's destitute widow a letter of condolence which read, in part, "I hope it will bring some comfort to know that the thoughts and prayers of the entire American Embassy community are with you and your family at this difficult time."

That was it. No check, no cash, no movie passes. Nothing. This slight, as you can imagine, enraged the global Internet community anew, which is no mean feat considering how angry everyone already was at the Embassy's deafening silence.

23 **"No comment" is no longer an option. If the story is about you, you have to be a part of it. You cannot let others tell your story for you.**

Great Beginnings, Happy Endings and Everything in Between

It's true that the Internet has changed the way we communicate both off- and online. But a good story still needs a strong opening and a dynamic close. They just need to be stronger and dynamic-er.

More dynamic.

Right. So let's start with the beginning.

24 **If you want people to listen to your story, you must hit them with your best information immediately.**

Unfortunately, too many communications professionals treat their leads like the prettiest present under the Christmas tree … and don't get to them until the end.

Take our friends at the Centre for Addiction and Mental Health, located in beautiful Toronto, Canada.

In 2012, the Centre uncovered some stop-the-presses news in their annual survey of substance abuse trends. According to their research, young people in Ontario were 30 percent more likely to smoke dope than drink alcohol before driving. Thirty percent!

But in their typical we're-so-nice-you-can't-help-but-like-us Canadian way, they led with good news, only *alluding* to "several areas of concern."

> **For Immediate Release – November 28, 2012 – (Toronto) – Most adults are drinking responsibly, and fewer are smoking or using illicit substances – but several areas of concern were found in the 2011 CAMH Monitor survey of Ontario substance use trends, released today by the Centre for Addiction and Mental Health (CAMH).**

And when they finally did get around to the good stuff, they reported it thus:

Nine per cent of 18- to 29-year-olds report driving after cannabis use, versus six per cent in this age range who report drinking two or more drinks and driving.

Soft as a baby's skull.

A much better headline would have been, *"Young people in Ontario are 30 percent more likely to smoke dope than drink alcohol before driving."*

Remember: You can't bury your lead. You must put the most important point you have in the first sentence, and write it in a way that locks eyeballs onto the screen.

"But what if what you have to say isn't eyeball-locking" you ask? Great question. Simple answer: Don't bother saying it.

They don't call it a climax for nothing: How to satisfy your audience with a powerful ending

"Even if you write a captivating beginning and an interesting middle, readers will want to hurl your book across the room and never buy another one of your novels if the ending doesn't satisfy." –Ylva Publishing

"Stop your worryin'. Chase said there is no chance in Hell they would end the show with th—"

Capturing your audience is just the start of the battle. Just as with rock concerts, fireworks displays, and full-body massages, you can't have a great story without a great ending.

Think of the climax as your gift to the audience for all they've endured to get to the end of the story. Whether sitting through an entire season of *Dallas* to learn who shot JR or simply sitting cross-legged until the end of *Lost in Space* before running to the bathroom, the audience deserves something for its patience.

They've done their part, so you've got to do yours. But how? Here are two resources that should prove helpful.

The first is a well-thought-out tutorial by Ylva Publishing (http://ylvapublishing.wordpress.com). The post, entitled "Satisfying endings," skillfully guides the reader from the *climax*—"the highest point of tension and action," to the *denouement*, another French word which, roughly translated, means "Thanks. I'll call you."

It's worth a read … and maybe even a cigarette.

But the most instructive tutorial on the importance of a good ending can be found in a video of the 2010 Disclosure Conference at the National Press Club (http://www.youtube.com/watch?v=3jUU4Z8QdHI). It's long (an hour and change), but the stories are riveting. And the endings are abysmal.

I can state with certainty that you will *never* encounter worse endings than these, which is amazing because these stories are riveting—the eye-witness accounts of aliens hovering over nuclear missile silos and deactivating the nukes—and they're being told by *the former Air Force officers who commanded those missile silos!*

In their defense, these guys were probably as surprised that they were speaking at a national news briefing as they were about their close encounters with aliens. And possibly even more frightened by it. But even cutting them that slack, these are without a doubt the most horrendous endings on some of the most amazing stories of all time.

Take the time to watch video. Study each ending closely. And then do the opposite when it's your turn to tell a story.

Until then, here are some simple tips to improve your endings:

 "Begin with the end in mind." Any good story goes through unexpected permutations as it's being developed, which is a natural and good thing. But one thing should remain constant: the ending. As Yogi Berra wisely said, "If you don't know where you're going, you might not get there."

Foreshadowing – It's important to offer smalls references in the body of the story to the element(s) that are crucial to the end.

Careful foreshadowing – It's also risky. The foreshadowing has to be done in a way that does not telegraph the knockout punch.

25 **Brevity is the soul of wit – The two most important elements of any story are the beginning and the end. The closer together you put these two critical elements, the better your story will be.**

As Kurt Vonnegut said, "Start as close to the end as possible."

Stay stoic, my friend. If the story you're telling ends with a laugh, do not laugh. That's almost as bad as saying, "I've got a funny story for you." Let your audience be the judge."

When you're done, you're done. Dénouements are for novelists and overachievers. When you made your point, stop talking.

Actually, John, while the dénouement might not be for everybody, it is actually a very helpful way to restate your quest in what is now a richer context for your audience.

Masterpiece Theatre: Connecting with your audience

The art of storytelling is often presented as a series of steps one must take to get from the beginning of a tale to the end, as if performing the *Hesitation Waltz*.

"Open, two, three ... setting, two, three ... character, two, three ... plot, two, three ..."

Master the steps and you've mastered storytelling. Except you haven't.

26 Great storytelling, like great dancing, is an art that requires an almost spiritual connection with your partner, the audience.

You can master the moves, but unless you can interpret and adjust to the subtle—sometimes nearly imperceptible—reactions of your audience to your story, you're not a storyteller. You're an iPod.

Naturally empathetic people are particularly good at reading their audience, as if they were born with exquisitely tuned radar. On the other end of the spectrum are sociopaths, whose radars were never properly installed. Most people fall somewhere in between.

It can be a bit much, as you can imagine, picking up subtle physical cues that tell you much more about someone's genuine state of mind than they want you to know. And constantly (yet subtly) adjusting your presentation can be exhausting, really. But it is an invaluable trait that has helped—and created—brilliant storytellers for generations.

"I know what you're thinking, and I swear to God my hand just slipped."

Here's a trick that will help you connect with your audience right away: Think of your story as a gift to your audience. Literally.

- **Select the perfect story for your audience**. Give them the story they want to hear, not (necessarily) the story you want to tell.

- **Give them the gift they want by making sure it's the right color and size**. A blue story might work well with the International Longshoremen's Association, but others—say the Mother Teresa Society—may feel compelled to refuse it. As to size, no one ever complained about a gift story being too short.

- **Cut off the price tag**. No one wants to hear you boast about your wonderful gift by laughing at your own story. If it was rich in humor, they will know, and they will thank you with laughs of their own.

- **And remember, the best gifts are homemade**. Know your material but be animated and flexible with the presentation. A canned, plastic, one-size-fits-all story told the same way every time doesn't mean nearly as much as a story that you crafted especially with your audience in mind.

27 **Preparation increases your chances of communicating effectively.**

"Bring Your Own BEER?! I've always understood it to mean 'Bring Your Own Boy.' Dreadfully sorry, old chap."

With the meteoric rise in sanctioned (and unsanctioned) videotaping of live performances, your off-the-cuff remarks in a gathering may well haunt you for years to come. And since many of the same tips will help you communicate via video, there's more reason than ever to master the art of the in-person presentation.

What's My Line: **Preparing a (loose) script**

If you're in the communications game, you've quite likely developed talking points for yourself and/or others or you wouldn't be reading this book. That level of preparation is sufficient in order to convey information; however, if you want to *communicate*, you need to put in a bit more work than merely memorizing a list of arguments and stats.

Instead, approach your upcoming communication as a jazz performance. There is an underlying baseline of information that you want to convey, but you'll embroider improvisation and on-the-spot interaction around that information to make your performance spontaneous and unique to the event.

It's also helpful to be current and relevant. Before any speech, we always:

- Check the day's headline to find *relevant* news to open with;

- Run a search on the group we are addressing (and their board if appropriate) to see if they have had recent publicity; and

- Confer with our hosts to see if there is any news or information about members of the audience that we could use in our presentation.

Another way to get some pre-performance intel is to get there early and talk to people. Talk to the staff, mingle with the audience, introduce yourself to the people eating breakfast, *etc.* It can be a bit daunting (especially if you're shy), but it usually pays dividends when the time comes to interact more formally.

One basic benefit is that you can identify a few familiar faces in the crowd. You can also reference discussions that you had with attendees, which shows some spontaneity and helps to particularize your remarks. And the people you already interacted with are more likely to pay attention and participate in your talk.

Extreme Makeover: The importance of non-verbal communication

Much of what your audience takes in—and reacts to both in person and via video—is *not* the words you say.

28 They are looking at your clothes, posture, and facial expressions. And they are making judgments about you, your issue, and your organization based on what they see.

One of the most common ways that people judge you is by what you're wearing. Clothes matter; take some time to dress thoughtfully.

In a room full of bankers, for example, showing up in jeans and a blazer will send an entirely different message than an impeccably tailored suit. Do you want to blend in or stand out? Make a conscious decision and dress accordingly.

29 Making an effort to create an outfit that supports your persona will help you get in character while also lending a visual interpretation of the personality you're trying to convey.

Let's get visual

Whether it's the parent holding a snapshot of a lost child or Netanyahu using a bomb graphic to draw attention to Iran's nuclear program, visuals draw attention.

Research has shown that people process images far more rapidly than they can absorb text, so peppering your speech with visuals and props actually makes it easier for your audience to pay attention and connect with what you're saying. Take advantage of this by incorporating pictures, charts, and visual props in your communications.

Or just pictures. After years of fighting it, I am now embracing my dyslexia. So every presentation I create is comprised of just pictures—no more words, no more charts, no more bullets. ("No more buwwets?" Anybody?)

The pictures serve two purposes. First, they remind me what I plan to say next. More often than not, I memorize these picture prompts so I can speak without a script. But when I do need to use notes, I print a thumbnail of the pictures next to the text.

More important, though, is the entertainment value of the pictures. To quote the brilliant David Thorne, "The Internet is a playground." You can find a picture of *ANYTHING* online. The trick is to use your imagination.

(If you're not already following David Thorne, do yourself the favor. Start at his blog—www.27bslash6.com—then buy his books. You will thank me.)

For example, when discussing connecting with your audience, I could use the universal default of the monochrome round-headed characters that find themselves in countless mind-numbing presentations. Or I could use a photo of an infant high-fiving a Siberian tiger through a Plexiglas wall.

"But how the hell am I going to find a picture like that?"

Good question. What I do is think of a different way to characterize the point I am trying to make and then enter search terms related to *that* topic. In this case, instead of Googling "connect with your audience," I Googled "Namaste," which essentially means "the spirit in me honors the spirit in you."

It's also helpful to use pictures of living things—people, animals, most celebrities—anything with eyes. These photos are infinitely more compelling than pictures of things. And it's a lot easier to find a picture of someone doing something humiliating than it is to find, say, a chair embarrassing itself.

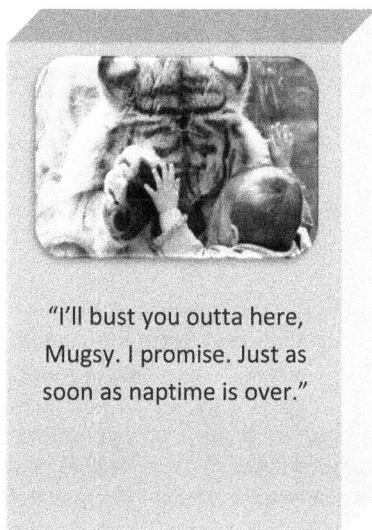

"I'll bust you outta here, Mugsy. I promise. Just as soon as naptime is over."

You should preset your search criteria so that the results contain just large pictures—a minimum of 600 x 600 pixels. The advanced search options also let you search for certain color photos, even the type of photo, such as photos with faces, line drawings, or clip art.

Stand up straight

Your mother was totally right about this one. Harvard psychologist Amy Cuddy has found that how we stand and sit not only affects how others perceive us, but also changes our own stress levels, assertiveness, and charisma. Striking "power poses" before and during presentations has been shown to lower cortisol levels and increase testosterone—two physiological changes that have been linked with better performance.

What constitutes a power pose? They are associated with openness, expansiveness, and dominance. Generally speaking, the more space you occupy, the better. Sitting with your feet up on the table and hands behind your head, standing in a "Wonder Woman" pose (feet apart and hands on your hips), or standing with your hands on the table all show confidence and dominance. Slumping, crossing your arms, and fidgeting, on the other hand, are considered "low power" actions, since they signal powerlessness or submission.

So before your next interview, videotaping, or speech, take a few minutes to (privately) strike a power pose. And watch how you hold yourself when you're communicating—because everyone else is watching, too.

"Stop me if you've heard me laugh at this one before."

Laughing at you own stories is like driving your new Porche through your friend's front door. You've wrecked a good thing and nobody appreciates what you've done. But don't take my word for it. Here's what Mark Twain had to say:

"The humorous story is told gravely; the teller does his best to conceal the fact that he even dimly suspects that there is anything funny about it; but the teller of the comic story tells you beforehand that it is one of the funniest things he has ever heard, then tells it with eager delight, and is the first person to laugh when he gets through. And sometimes, if he has had good success, he is so glad and happy that he will repeat the 'nub' of it and glance around from face to face, collecting applause, and then repeat it again. It is a pathetic thing to see."

Reno 911!: **Responding to Communications "Incidents"**

Recovering from a gaffe

So what do you do when faced with that dreadful moment when your mind goes blank? Having a recovery prop is invaluable.

A glass of water is the simplest and most versatile recovery prop, and many speakers make certain to have a glass (and a pitcher) of water nearby. A moment of confusion can easily be disguised by taking a sip of water or refilling your glass, with the added benefit that you ease a constricted throat and dampen a dry mouth. A cup of coffee or tea can serve the same purpose and also convey a soothing warmth.

The three most powerful words

No, not "I love you." Not in this context, anyway. They are "I don't know."

Along with attempting to be perfect, many people try to answer every question. When you're the center of attention, there's a strong impulse to show that you know what you're talking about at all times, even if it means giving a lame or incorrect answer.

(And this is not me lecturing—I struggle with this frequently. Under pressure, I tend to feel that admitting that I don't know the answer to *everything* calls into question whether I know *anything*. I've found myself meandering in the forest of "stuff pulled out of thin air" more than once. In those situations, I try to dig myself out of trouble with "But that's just my opinion; I can't speak authoritatively about this subject." But sometimes I just have to say, "You know what? Upon reflection, I don't know the answer.")

But when you say "I don't know," you create rapport with your audience. You're no longer the teacher lecturing them; you're a person who is fallible and imperfect. You are showing vulnerability, and the natural human reaction is to feel closer to someone after such an experience.

You can further draw in the crowd by asking "Do any of you know the answer?" If someone knows the answer, it's a great way to include them in the "performance." If no one does, the fact that you don't know has become a trait that you share with your audience.

If it's something that can be learned, you might say "I don't know, but I will find out." Depending on the circumstance, you could add "And then I'll get back to you." This opens up channels for ongoing communications and gives you the chance to demonstrate trustworthiness by keeping your promise.

Bringing "sorry" back

"I am sorry" is also a powerful word trio, but a lot of people still don't know how to handle that verbal weapon. Compare FOX Network's Shepard Smith and Doping Network's Lance Armstrong—two apologizers who are on opposite ends of the *mea culpa* continuum.

When FOX inadvertently broadcast live coverage of a fatal shot at the end of a car chase, Shep immediately apologized, explained how the screw-up occurred, took personal responsibility for it, and pledged that it "won't happen again on my watch."

A solid 10 on the sorry spectrum. In the apology game, Smith is your Shepard.

Lance, on the other hand, didn't have the … the courage to own up to years of doping, lying, and bullying until he saw a chance to cop a plea with his *mea culpa*.

Lance gets a 1. Just 1. And some of the judges think he should lose that one, too.

You're going to screw up someday. Trust me. When you do, take the hit as a gift. The manner in which you accept (or don't accept) responsibility for your actions will define you. It will enrich your story—for better or for worse. So do the right thing. Take responsibility. Apologize. And promise to not do it again.

Folks'll love you for it.

Firing Line: Dealing with disagreement

The power of preserving silence is the very first requisite to all who wish to shine, or even please in discourse; and those who cannot preserve it, have really no business to speak. ... This is the really eloquent silence. It requires great genius—more perhaps than speaking—and few are gifted with the talent ...

—Martine's Hand-book of Etiquette, and Guide to True Politeness

Generally speaking, you'll face three basic kinds of disagreement:

1. Disagreement based on ignorance or misinformation
2. Disagreement based on ideological differences
3. Opportunistic troublemakers (AKA "trolls" or "bomb throwers")

Since it can be difficult to identify the kind of engagement you are about to have, use a cumulative method with increasing disengagement.

A good defense is not offensive

Chances are excellent that you know far more about your industry, organization, or issue than most of the people you meet. So the most common form of disagreement you'll face is based on faulty information.

In these cases, empathy and respect are your best tools. These are people who made judgments based on the information that they had. But the very act of forming that opinion required an emotional investment. So logic alone is unlikely to be effective.

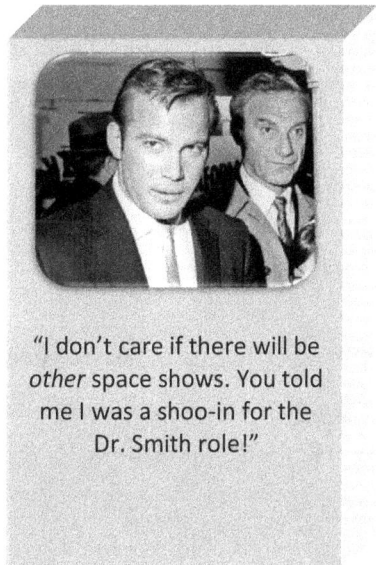

"I don't care if there will be *other* space shows. You told me I was a shoo-in for the Dr. Smith role!"

Instead, combine logic with a true attempt to get to the bottom of the misconception that fuels their disagreement. Showing respect for them and their views creates a basis of trust for you to share information or correct falsehoods, with the result that the person can now see the issue "in a new light."

No one likes to be wrong. The more effectively you can move your discussion from right v. wrong to "I never thought of it that way," the more likely you are to persuade that person.

You'd be amazed what a simple statement like "I totally understand why you think that" can help move a discussion from combative to informative.

Different strokes for different folks

When the disagreement that you are facing is based not (just) on false or misguided information but is also driven by a fundamentally different belief system, there's almost no chance that you'll be able to persuade them.

In these cases, the person's opinion is an outgrowth of a worldview or philosophy, rather than just a set of facts that they used to make a decision. In order for them to change their mind, they would have to alter—even if minutely—their belief system. And while that's not impossible, it is certainly far more difficult to accomplish than merely correcting misinformation.

Situations like these are apt to get more heated, since by disagreeing with their opinion you are calling their beliefs into question. They will most likely take it personally and express some hostility towards you.

The likelihood of changing minds is slim; the likelihood of the disagreement escalating is quite high. Your best strategy is to defuse the situation by acknowledging their right to hold different opinions and agree to disagree.

When trouble is its own reward

Then there's the opportunistic troublemakers who foment discord for their own gain.

They might be looking for publicity or attention from others, but the motivation is unimportant. The relevant point is that there is no productive way to engage with someone who is intent on disagreeing in an insulting and disrespectful way. Any attention you give them is unlikely to benefit you, so try to extricate yourself from the exchange as quickly as possible. Remain polite but feel free to refrain from expressing respect for their opinions when you are dealing with this kind of toxic situation.

Eight Simple Rules: A short summary for the short-attention-span set

Just as "age is a state of mind," so is successful storytelling. Even more so because—and I speak from experience—age is more than a state of mind. It's a sore back, Prilosec, and a perpetual search for my reading glasses.

But to go with the conceit, here are three simple things you can do to engage your audience:

- Stay in character.

- Never patronize your audience.

- Be passionate.

And for those of you with the capacity to read more, here are some stories to help bring these rules to life.

1) Stay in character.

Back in 2012 not long after Facebook bought it for $1 billion, Instagram announced plans to share its users photos with advertisers, "in some cases without notice or compensation," as *TIME* magazine explained.

The uproar that followed wasn't just because selling people's photos was a clown move, but because we had all come to love and trust Instagram. A lot of beliefs were shattered when we learned that Instagram was really about making a profit.

2) Never patronize your audience.

When Netflix split itself into two companies in 2011, thereby requiring their customer base to pay up to 60 percent more for less streamlined service, the Netflix community went nuts. Netflix CEO Reed Hastings did a quick 180 on the new model, and the offered one of the phoniest apology videos the world has ever seen.

Following is what he said, followed by what most of us heard:

"We're making this video today to apologize in person, or at least on camera, for something that we did recently."

"The boys at the firm say this gag works better than roses. A veritable get-out-of-jail-free card."

"When we communicated [our plan] to our subscribers—and it involves a substantial price increase for most members—I didn't make the communication and we didn't explain why we were doing it."

"'Substantial' in little air quotes. I mean, it's a couple of bucks. You just got your panties in a twist because I didn't tell you in person. Well, here I am!"

"If I had communicated it directly to all of our members, it wouldn't change the actual price increase."

"So what's really got you down? Is it a lady thing?"

"To wrap up, I just want to say again how sorry I am of the way that we handled the communication around these big changes."

"So wipe your eyes, sweetheart. Daddy's sorry for his tone. Now, be a doll and fix me a drink, will ya?"

3)   Be passionate.

YouTube is the Lee Strasberg of social media platforms. It will force you to become a more convincing, more passionate storyteller, or it will wash you out of the game. Because when it comes to video, passionate conviction gets shared; dispassionate convention gets shelved.

Take the infectiously viral video of Sen. Kirsten Gillibrand (D-NY) upbraiding, down dressing, and generally sidelining the judge advocate general of the Air Force, Lt. Gen. Richard Harding, for refusing to answer her question about whether "justice was done" when one Air Force jet-fighter officer unilaterally overturned the rape conviction of another Air Force jet-fighter officer. Her rage was intense and her performance was riveting.

"Brace yourself, Fly Boy. You're about to be Gilli-branded!"

After being convicted of aggravated sexual assault, Lt. Colonel James Wilkerson was sentenced to a year in the brig. But rather than go to jail, he went back to work when his boss, Air Force Commander Lt. Gen. Craig Franklin, declared the conviction null and void. Sen. Gillibrand, as you can imagine, was less than amused.

But you will be amused by her grilling of Harding on this issue. And, once again, you will learn another important lesson in captivating storytelling at someone else's expense: To tell a remarkable story in the YouTube age, it pays to be passionate.

Key Points

- Your staff is already talking about your organization and your issues. But they may not be doing it well.
- Preparation increases your chances of communicating effectively.
- No one is as good without preparation as they are with it. So make it a priority.
- Your audience won't remember most of what you say.
- Appearances matter.
- Spoiler alert: you're going to screw up. So prepare ahead of time for how you'll handle mistakes in high-pressure, public situations.
- No good presentation has ever resulted from reading text off of PowerPoint slides. Interact with your audience.
- It's not going to go perfectly. Ever.
- For every point of view, someone else holds the opposite view—just as fervently.

Live your story

Home Improvement: The mechanics of your organization's "show"

There was a time when we got our information from the morning newspaper and the 6 o'clock news. But on June 1, 1980, Ted Turner launched *CNN* and put an end to that quaint news-delivery system. This new cable news show required a fundamental rethinking of what constituted news and how other news channels (and other entertainment channels, for that matter) functioned.

As news expanded from a public service to entertainment programming, it underwent some interesting changes and spawned new ways to gather and deliver the news. They include:

- Immediate responses to events
- A perpetual focus on content development
- The need for "guest experts," partners, and other voices
- Increased audience participation
- Regularly scheduled shows and over-the-horizon planning

These changes are among the many that organizations around the globe are applying to their communication strategies in the Interactive Age. And they are among the changes you must adopt as well, if you want to survive and thrive in this brave new world.

Sounds like a lot of work, doesn't it? It's a not inconsiderable adjustment. But remember, as you incorporate 21st century tactics into your communications strategy, you'll also eliminate a lot of inefficient and ineffective 20th century tasks.

> And, quite frankly, these adjustments are not optional. Just as you had to learn to type, send email, and post on Facebook, you are going to have to learn how to manage your own communications production company. And like learning email, it will take some time to adjust. But the rewards will be well worth the effort.

You'll also find productivity and resources coming from unexpected sources and ongoing technological advances. Most importantly, the responsibility for telling and living your organization's story will naturally spread from its traditional wheelhouse—the communications and marketing departments—and will be picked up by others in your organization.

And it can also be fun. It *should* be fun. With the fall of the fourth wall came the fall of perfection. In fact, slick productions send the wrong message. Audiences today appreciate vulnerability and personality more than the perfect recitation of statistics. So let them get to know the people behind the product or idea—you might be surprised at how enjoyable it can be to interact with strangers.

So what do you do first? I've found that the best way to succeed is to learn from those who already have succeeded … Like Ted Leonsis.

Ted Leonsis is an incredibly successful businessman. He owns the Washington Wizards basketball team and the Washington Capitals hockey team and is a wizard at capitalizing on opportunities. For example, in 2013 Leonsis retooled the "decades-old business model" of his media and sports empire to take advantage of 21st century technology. And he didn't undertake this overhaul to survive. He did it to thrive.

According to *The Washington Post,* Leonsis' company "is going aggressively digital, asking employees to broaden their skill sets, collaborate more, produce extra content and find innovative ways to deliver it." One sentence, five lessons. Take note; they are meant for you.

Go aggressively digital: Your organization's online presence isn't "another tool in our communications toolbox." It's the whole job site. As Ted says: "We believe in the three-screen future. There's the computer. There's the phone, and then there's television." You've got to get online if you want to get your story on those screens.

Ask employees to broaden their skill sets: That content assembly line that allowed every department to add its own tweak to each press release? Scrap it. Online conversations happen in real time. Your team needs to have the skills—and the authority—to communicate in real time for your story to be part of the story.

Collaborate more: The online culture is collaborative. Want your story to be retold by communities you care about? Start by engaging in the conversation. If you bust into a group of like-minded folk having a friendly conversation and you start handing out press releases, you will get talked about. But you won't like what you hear.

Produce extra content: To paraphrase Brad Pitt's character in *Inglourious Basterds*, "The Internet ain't in the press-release posting business. It's in the content-sharing business. And, cousin, business is a-BOOMin." Content is the currency of the Internet. But your content must be current—and that takes constant upkeep. So as your employees are broadening their skill sets, encourage the more conversant of them to engage in online conversations on behalf of the organization. (Don't forget to give them the authority to keep those conversations alive without running everything by legal.)

Find innovative ways to deliver content: Rod McKuen had it right: "The medium is the message." But online media is much more than blogs, tweets, and like. One of the best ways to deliver content is by engaging in other people's conversations. See a blog post you like that is relevant to your issue? Leave a comment. Come across a podcast that offers a unique take on a topic you care about? Share it on Facebook. Before long, others will return the favor and you'll be part of the conversation.

WKRP in Cincinnati: Building your own "control booth"

TV shows aren't created for the producers' psychic satisfaction. They are created to make money, just as your organization likely was (at least enough money to pursue your quest). And much like a TV producer, you have a distinct audience you want to reach, with specific information you want to convey, to obtain well-defined results. Unfortunately, just as in TV, that process is rather more complicated than it has ever been, and it requires daily coordination, production, and monitoring.

So how do you go about establishing a virtual control booth, where you can run the daily effort involved in producing, distributing, and evaluating your organization's TV show?

Start with the old-school journalistic standards: Who? What? Where? When? Why? (The details of your organization will dictate a highly specific "how," so it will not be covered here.)

For each area, we'll look at some tactics, tips, and tools you can use.

Who? Finding and building your audience

As we previously discussed, it all starts with your audience. Much like with a TV show, you should put in a great deal of thought regarding who *precisely* you are trying to reach with your organization's story.

Remember: content is a consumers' market. You want to communicate with your target audience far more than they want to interact with you. Add in the millions of other messages competing for their attention every day, and you've got a challenge if you want to recruit, retain, and grow an audience for your metaphorical TV show.

Strategies and Tactics

1) Cheat off the smart kid
While your organization is unique, it likely shares the field with others in the same area. So save yourself some time and trouble and check out what your competitors are doing.

Make a list of individuals and organizations with quests similar to yours, and do some research on the following:

- Which platforms are they using to communicate? Which of those are the most successful?
- What story are they telling, and how is it being received?
- Who is drawn to their efforts? Who is challenging them?

Also look at organizations in other areas that are doing a great job of communicating with their audiences. What common traits do you notice? Can they be adapted to your efforts?

Here's an example that demonstrates the best and worst communications tactics in one debate.

Xcel Energy—a privately-held power company—fought for its very existence against *New Era Colorado*—a band of dedicated environmentalists who declared they were "on the verge of setting an important precedent that has national significance and could threaten not just Xcel Energy but the very core of the business model, and the billions of dollars in profit that come with it, of the dirty coal energy industry."

Considering the reaction from Xcel—and the energy utility industry in general—they may be right.

In 2011, the people of Boulder, CO voted to wrest control of the power grid from Xcel and become a locally owned utility. Xcel fought back by getting an initiative on the 2013 ballot that would scuttle the deal if it were to pass, setting up a showdown that will have profound repercussions for the utilities industry if Xcel were to lose (which they did … in a landslide).

The reason? *New Era Colorado* got the jump on Xcel with a well-produced video that laid out their case for why voters in Boulder should not overturn the 2011 election results.

Upworthy, a website for viral content, posted the video and urged people to share it. *Huff Post* picked up the story and—to no one's surprise—the video went viral. Big time. The goal of the video was to crowd-source $40,000 in two weeks. They raised $197,000. Their opposition spent three times that amount, with half of that money coming from Xcel.

Adding to Xcel's pain was the revelation in the video that their communications effort included a "textbook" published by the Edison Electric Institute that Xcel and other utilities are using to fight the growing movement to localize power supplies. The advice included:

- "Develop fact sheets and other information you can leave behind";
- "Feature charitable activities in bill inserts"; and
- Establish a website because "increasingly, individuals are turning to the Internet for political information."

As we've learned with the Yellow Pages, Blockbuster Video, and the United States Postal Service—to name just a few—it's a brave new world out there. You have to adapt or you will die.

30 The days of talking *to* are over. You now must communicate *with* your partners, honestly and transparently.

2) Fish Where the Fish Are

Different types of people congregate on different online platforms in order to get different kinds of information. Learn about the differences between social media platforms, and pay attention to how the users change over time. It may be appropriate to focus your attention on Facebook at present, but next year your audience might be somewhere else entirely.

3) Reciprocate

This one is hard to overstate. The Golden Rule that you learned in kindergarten—namely, "treat others the way you would like to be treated"—should guide pretty much all of your social media actions. If someone follows you, follow them back (after checking that they aren't spammers). If someone promotes your info, thank them … and ideally promote something of theirs in the near future. It needn't be on the same platform—for instance, if someone likes your Facebook post, reciprocate by retweeting their material. This helps to build relationships across platforms and also makes it clear that you aren't just mindlessly mirroring their actions.

4) Be human

For those who are transitioning from "old school" communications, making yourself vulnerable, admitting mistakes, and asking for help are extremely uncomfortable. But if you think of a social media platform as a cocktail party or picnic, the rationale behind this tactic becomes clear. We've all been stuck with that guy who pontificates endlessly. And we've all had the pleasure of feeling like the smartest person in the room when someone asks our opinion or admits their ignorance. So make your case and convey your information. But also listen to others, ask questions, and don't feel ashamed to say "I was wrong."

Tips

- **Start with the low-hanging fruit.** These may be suppliers, clients, supporters, industry groups, or other like-minded people. They are not only the most likely ones to be interested in what you have to say but also will serve as a nucleus for your community.
- **Track your audience across platforms.** If someone is interested in your organization on one platform, they'll likely engage on others. So if someone likes your Facebook page, check and see if they have accounts on the other platforms your organization uses (*e.g.,* Twitter, Instagram, LinkedIn). And follow those you wish to engage with on the platforms that they favor.
- **Prioritize your outreach efforts.** Pick a few key players to focus on and engage with them. Once you feel like you've got a "relationship" started, expand out to a few more people. Trying to bond with hundreds of people at once is a bit like speed dating—the chances that you'll make any impression at all are pretty slim when you're spreading yourself so thin.

Tools

There are a multitude of apps, programs, and tools that can help you grow your audience. Below are a few options to get you started:

- Tweepi (www.Tweepi.com) is very handy for growing your Twitter audience. It allows you to follow the followers and friends of other Twitter accounts, which is a fantastic way to identify people who are interested in your arena. You can also easily see their bio, number of friends/followers, and picture—which can all be helpful for eliminating or avoiding spammers. It lets you know who is following you that you are not yet following back, and who is not following you back. The paid options also allow you to unfollow people who haven't tweeted or reciprocated in a given time period, force spammers to unfollow you, see people's klout scores, *etc.*
- To help identify influencers in your area, check out blog rankings like those at http://technorati.com/blogs/directory/. Commenting on posts by popular authors is a great way to engage as well as find people to follow on other platforms.
- Check out the membership lists of industry associations.

- Use your location to expand your audience—engage with local Chambers of Commerce, nonprofits, neighborhood blogs, *etc.*
- If you set up a daily "paper" at Paper.li (covered below), the curated articles can be a great source of audience intel, both by looking at the original author and the people who shared their piece.

What? Creating content in a transmedia world

One of the common questions we hear is "How do I find enough stuff to say?"

First, a bit of reassurance. You're not expected to create enough original content to fill your content pipeline. In fact, a good portion of the information you share *shouldn't* be yours. Share relevant news, articles, posts, and reports from other sources. This kind of content curation yields benefits: the ongoing education you receive about issue developments and players, the value you can offer your audience through the selection of great content, and the opportunity to build relationships with the authors and organizations you are publicizing.

Moreover, a large portion of your effort should be put into reacting (and interacting) with what others are saying and sharing.

And just like a TV show, you can use "real world" events, classic storylines, and anniversaries as inspiration for your content.

Strategies and Tactics

The Internet never sleeps, so someone is always talking about your organization or issues. And unfortunately, "ignorance is bliss" is no longer a strategic option.

31   **It is incumbent on your organization to remain on top of current events, developments in your industry, and to keep a finger on the pulse of what people are saying about your organization on social media platforms.**

1) Develop keyword searches

There are very decent free online monitoring systems, as well as paid programs. Regardless of which you use, they are only as good as the keywords that you are monitoring. So create a couple different lists of terms and then monitor the differences in the results. This can help ensure that you are using the most efficient terms.

Your terms might include:

- Your organization's name and the names of your products or issues (both domestic and international)
- The names of your competitors and allies (both organization names and the leaders or key spokespeople)
- Industry or organizational terminology
- Areas of local, state, and/or federal government regulation or legislation

Depending upon the size of your staff and the level of your investment, you might divide these searches (either by keyword or by platform) among different departments or people, asking that they share the most relevant articles and posts each day. This also creates a great pipeline for your content curation efforts. You'll be surprised at the amount of foreshadowing you will see once it becomes an organizational routine.

It's also amazing how much information and research your staff will come across while searching for relevant material to post on social media. Encouraging them to pass around this material helps establish what is functionally an in-house research department.

Discontent Is King

You'd be amazed at how many nonprofit organizations—and for-profit companies, for that matter—still employ a one-shot-a-month *Guns of Navarone* communications strategy.

For these organizations, putting out a press release is a rare and momentous achievement. The fact that the press release didn't generate any press is inconsequential. The kids in public affairs have done it again—they put out a press release!

So it shouldn't surprise anyone that these organizations are being outgunned on the Internet by millions of relentless communicators who fire every weapon they can scrounge up and seize every opportunity they can find—or create—to tell their story.

These content ninjas are never satisfied, never relaxed. They are constantly on the prowl for ideas, inspiration, and intelligence that will entertain and engage their audience. Posting a blog entry doesn't fulfill them. It just reduces their discomfort a little, like scratching a mosquito bite through a combat boot.

And that's why those guys are kicking ass.

A lot of organizations are closing in on these communications warriors. Press releases announcing the "recently hired Chief Content Officer"—a new position— are lighting up the Internet like tracer rounds.

These shiny new CCOs have a tough mission: they must mold every facet of their company into a storytelling battalion or the victories will be few. But they also have a lot of motivation—the future of their organization depends on them.

Yes, a good CCO is that important.

2) Relate your quest to bigger or current issues

In our fast-moving and cluttered information-based society, it's unreasonable to expect that your organization is going to often (or ever) be at the top of the news cycle. So learning how to tie in, adapt around, and build upon other events is a crucial skill in keeping a content stream flowing. And in this area, using your organization's quest is an invaluable starting point.

Here are a few tips:

Scope it up or down. It's easy to get stuck in a self-created rut, so ask yourself:

- What cultural, environmental, or economic obstacles do you face in achieving your quest?

- Do you have a unique perspective on them or their impact?
- What other problems are being caused by these same obstacles?
- Who is benefitting from or getting hurt by these obstacles?

This series of questions should help bring to mind a number of larger, tangential issues where your organization can share expertise, offer opinions, or provide a new angle.

In order to "scope it down," ask yourself:

- Do you know of any individual or group that has benefitted from your work?
- Are there individuals or groups that are or would be especially affected by the problem that you hope to solve/prevent?
- Do you have a perspective on how a county, state, federal, foreign, or international issue affects individuals or groups?
- How does your quest play out at the local and individual levels?

Identify your "issue ripples"

To help you organize your issues, imagine them as "ripples in the ponds" of your audiences' minds. Put your most tightly and precisely defined quest in the middle and put your more tangential, secondary, or global aspects of your quest in the succeeding circles. Try moving them around a bit to see if you can make a coherent "flow" of issues. While opportunity will guide some of your decisions, you should prioritize communication of these issues based on their distance from the central quest. The more

"Careful, Doug! I've been having issues with that slippery ripple."

directly it relates, the more it should be at the forefront of your efforts.

3) Collaborate and compete

Look for quest alignment opportunities. Chances are, you aren't the only organization facing or trying to solve these problems, and that these problems cause or contribute to a multitude of other problems. So look for groups with complementary quests, or build coalitions out of diverse groups who happen to share an interest in one or more aspects of your quest. How can you partner with others to magnify your voice?

> In addition to increasing your firepower and base of support, the "team of rivals" approach is often a great story in itself. Not long after Edward Snowden let the world know that the National Security Agency was reading our emails and listening to our online chats, eight of the world's largest technology giants—which are also fierce rivals—joined forces to try to poke a stick into the NSA's prying eyes.
>
> In "an open letter to Washington," these tech giants demanded reforms that would restrict and oversee the government's surveillance of the governed. It was signed by AOL, LinkedIn, Facebook, Google, Twitter, Yahoo, Apple and Microsoft, one of the few instances where Microsoft and Apple's logo appeared side by side on something other than a legal brief.
>
> Partnering with rivals also sharpens the media's focus on the issue—if two swashbucklers temporarily drop their swords to work together on an issue, that issue becomes much more interesting to the crowd watching the sword fight. Here are a couple of examples we've had a hand in over the years:
>
> - Sen. George McGovern, former democratic candidate for president in 1972, penned several op-eds warning Congress of the unintended consequences of heavy-handed wage and health mandates.
>
> - MADD Founder Candy Lightner did numerous media interviews in which she urged lawmakers to oppose efforts to lower the drunk driving arrest threshold and focus instead on the real source of the drunk driving problem: alcohol abusers.
>
> - Steve Brobeck, the executive director of the Consumer Federation

of America, and Ron O'Hanley, president and CEO of Bank of New York Mellon Asset Management, shared the podium at a national news conference where they both called on banks to offer more incentives for people to increase their personal savings.

Similarly, think about legislation, natural disasters, or economic trends that effect or are affected by your quest. How can you contribute an interesting perspective or inform the larger debate?

Hurricanes seem to whip up people's generosity and creativity. Here are three organizations that highlighted their generosity (and their products and services!) following several massively destructive hurricanes:

- **Sharing a [Dasani] and a smile after Hurricane Katrina**—In the wake of the hurricane that destroyed much of New Orleans, the American Beverage Association, working with their member companies, mobilized a caravan of over 100 trucks to deliver fresh water to the storm victims.

- **Lessons learned after Hurricane Sandy thanks to the AASA**— After Hurricane Sandy destroyed entire towns—and the schools that served them—the Superintendents Association (ASSA) built a national online network that connected school districts in need with school districts around the country that had school supplies to give.

- **Cleaning up after Hurricane Isaac**—Proctor & Gamble's massive product empire allowed them to create and deliver three vitally important services for the victims of Hurricane Isaac. They dispatched their *Tide Loads of Hope* trucks, where people could drop off dirty laundry and have it washed, dried, and folded for free. They set up countless *Charmin Restrooms* (for obvious reasons). And they dispatched their *Duracell Rapid Responder* centers that allowed people to charge their devices, borrow computers, and share their Wi-Fi.

- **And from the "learning from others' mistakes" file** comes a lesson on exactly how NOT to contribute "an interesting perspective" on a natural disaster. Hours after thousands lost their homes, their towns, and their loved ones to Hurricane Sandy, American Apparel sent out an email announcing a 36-hour sale "in case you're bored during the storm." Appropriate public shaming ensued.

Find your line(s) in the sand. Anyone on a quest faces opponents and obstacles. Who and what are yours? Why do you disagree with these people or ideas? What "common knowledge" do you know to be wrong or incomplete?

In particular, being clear about not only what you stand *for* but also what you stand *against* creates opportunities for telling your story. These include:

- Responding to, explaining, and/or correcting erroneous or misguided content. (While there is an appalling amount of unproven, misleading, or outright untrue content out there, be extremely careful to verify the facts or anecdotes you use to debunk them. Your efforts will backfire if someone ends up debunking *you*.)
- Creating a dialogue with people of differing viewpoints, both to share your own story and to learn where there may be opportunities for persuasion or partnership.(If your organization can find a "sparring partner" on your issue, this opens up great opportunities to refine your story, work together for some form of a debate, debunk misconceptions, refer others to that group when they are looking for opposing views, *etc.*)
- Tracking news on your obstacle or opponents to identify additional angles for incorporating your story into existing conversations and debates.

Find "the rest of the story." Why is your quest worth pursuing? What do you know that would motivate others to change their mind or more strongly support your quest? What alternate perspective, arguments, or facts can you provide that most people don't know about your issue? By providing new material or insights, you create opportunities for people to change their minds without being "wrong" and give ammunition to your current supporters.

Always use your indoor voice on the Internet

While social media encourages collaboration and civility, social media tools encourage boundless ass-hattery. Much like cars.

It is a fascinating paradox of human nature that we would gladly hold open a tavern door for the person we just tried to kill in a moment of blinding road rage on our way to that tavern.

A lot of our rage behind the wheel is attributed to the anonymity that we enjoy in our cars—that and the fact that this jackhole has been driving 55 in the left lane with his blinker on for the last two miles and I swear to God if I ever get in front of him …

But I digress.

Social media is having much the same effect on our frontal lobes, allowing us to engage in behavior so unsociable that we wouldn't even confess it to our priest.

*Which leads to another quick digression. Before Monsignor Bulman excommunicated my mom from St. Mary's for having the gall to find herself divorced(!) from her philandering husband, she used to help us make up sins on the way to confession. It was only a two-mile ride, so there was a lot of frantic horse trading in the back of our station wagon.

"I don't want 'hitting.' I didn't hit anybody!"

"OK, I'll take 'hitting,' Mary Beth. But you gotta take 'being disrespectful' and 'skipping your prayers.'"

"But I *didn't* skip my prayers."

"Fine. We'll give that to Marnie. She needs some more sins anyway. But then you gotta take 'not sharing.'"

"But I *always* share!"

And although we never said it out loud, we all knew that making up sins to confess to the priest definitely

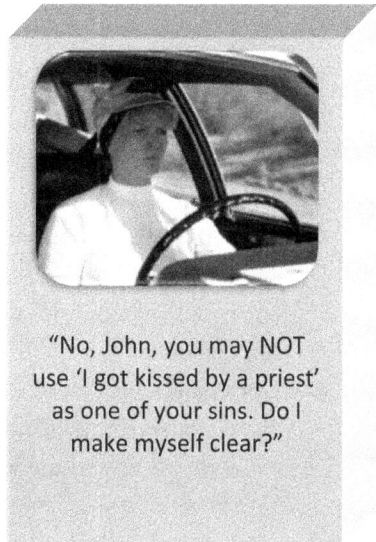

"No, John, you may NOT use 'I got kissed by a priest' as one of your sins. Do I make myself clear?"

qualified as one of the sins we should 'fess up to.

A rather spectacular example of unsocial media that resulted in "career Twittercide" involved one Jofi Joseph, aka @natsecwonk, who was an Obama political appointee to the National Security Council in 2013. Protected by the anonymity of his Twitter account, Joseph engaged in a self-described "series of inappropriate and mean-spirited comments" for more than two years.

When he was finally outed as the culprit in a sting orchestrated by White House officials, he was promptly fired, an administrative action that was confirmed by White House spokesman Jay Carney. Not a good day for Jofi. Not good at all.

So what can we learn from this, kids? Right. If you need to make snarky comments about your co-workers, your boss, or your employer, don't do it online, especially if you're a presidential appointee to the freakin' NSC. If you must complain, do it the old-fashioned way—in drunken slurs slumped over your seventh Jameson's neat in your favorite neighborhood tavern. And for God's sake, take a cab home.

Tips

- **It's OK to repeat yourself.** Social media posts are usually on others' screens for a few seconds, if at all. Use mechanisms such as ICYMI ("In case you missed it") tweets or a weekly compilation of "best reads" to repurpose and re-expose your audience to the content you've generated or curated.
- **Talk to yourself.** Take a moment to read your post or tweet aloud before sending it. Given the utter lack of context online, you can save yourself some grief by making sure that you're saying what you mean to say.
- **You will make mistakes.** With this level of content creation, I doubt you'll fully avoid typos, the prematurely posted piece, or erroneous/misleading statements. Fix it if you can, apologize if you can't, and move on.
- **Get visual.** Since people can absorb information through visuals more quickly and easily than by reading, there has been a concomitant rise in the visual conveyance of information

(infographics, animations, video, *etc.*). This trend will only increase as the supply of information continues to overwhelm the demand.

- **Source your facts.** Tracking down the original source of a statistic or factoid allows you to not only embed a link (thereby increasing your credibility) but will also give some indication as to the trustworthiness of that piece of information.

Tools

With the overwhelming amount of content flowing every minute of every day, filtering to exclude irrelevant informational noise becomes paramount. Here are a few tools that you can use to curate and compile content:

- Your blog is probably your major content hub. A user-friendly, endlessly customizable platform like Wordpress makes it easy to add plugins that help you write posts, optimize them for SEO, and make it easy for others to share.
- Tools like Evernote, which allow you to save and access text, articles, pictures, *etc.* across devices, can be extremely helpful for content generation. You can save a link from an article you read on your phone, add some notes from your tablet, and access it all from your laptop later.
- Social media management tools like Hootsuite allow you to create curated feeds based upon source, keyword, *etc.* This can be a great way to track and engage with others on your issues, and to help you in curating others' information for inclusion on your various platforms.
- News aggregators like Feedly and Flipboard compile blogs and news sites for easy reading, which streamlines the content curation process.
- Paper.li gives you the ability to create a daily "newspaper" based on topics and sources of your choosing. If you choose to automatically tweet each new edition, you will gain ancillary benefits from the generated list of authors who contributed "top stories." These people will often retweet, reply, or thank you for the inclusion.
- Newsle.com is a great way to keep track of important people in your organization, industry, and life. It compiles news, blog posts, and social media stories about (or by) your contacts and delivers a regular email to remind you to view them. These are great opportunities for reaching out or maintaining relationships.

- If you already have a well-established blog, you might consider using a plugin to tweet old posts—especially if your posts tend to be on evergreen topics.
- Last but not least, use extensions and plugins such as Buffer to make it easy for you to transform articles into social media posts with the click of a button.

Where and When? Planning your TV Season

Great content is a fantastic tool for telling your organization's story. But if you don't effectively disseminate it at the right times and places, it might as well not exist. So take some time to plan your "TV season" and to put protocols in place for dealing with the unexpected.

Strategies and Tactics

1) Create an editorial calendar

One of the most helpful ways to ensure that your story is being consistently incorporated is to make an editorial calendar. There are two main components that need to be considered: calendar-based opportunities and event-based opportunities.

A good portion of your content will be influenced by pre-scheduled occurrences. These include:

- Holidays
- Anniversaries
- The launch of new programs or reports
- Annual meetings
- Legislative calendars
- Historical events (the signing of Declaration of Independence, when women got the right to vote, the date that Prohibition was repealed, *etc.*)

Using a six- or 12-month window, start noting religious and civil holidays, known vacation times of key staff and upcoming events.

When you've exhausted your knowledge, share it with the rest of your organization. They will almost certainly have additions to make. Keep the final calendar accessible to relevant staff; it is not only a living document (being changed as more is known, dates are shifted, *etc.*) but also a helpful resource for coordinating activities across departments and assessing content flow.

2) Find Anniversaries

Once you start looking, you'll find that almost every day marks the birth or death of someone related to your issues; the anniversary of a significant development in your industry; or an event that you can tie into the messages that you're trying to convey.

To start with, take a gander at the sheer number of "National _____ Day/Week/Month" occasions there are. Many won't be appropriate, but mark down those that relate to your organization on your master calendar.

Then start thinking about significant people and events in your industry or issue area. Was there a famous scientist, president, or writer who has a connection to your organization? Mark down each person's birthday and death date.

It also behooves you to note down tragic anniversaries—the *Challenger* disaster, bombing of Pearl Harbor, *etc.*—so that they can be dealt with appropriately or knowingly avoided.

For a more temporal approach, you can search selected anniversaries for any given day on Wikipedia.

Making your own news

I loved playing lawn darts when I was a kid. The only thing that even came close to the thrill of throwing deadly weapons at each other was "arrow tag," which consisted of us standing around Billy Shoemaker as he shot an arrow straight up and then running around like blind mole rats to avoid getting hit when it came down. If you got hit, you were out—often for a very long time.

My sister Mary Beth really liked her Hoppity Hop. I wasn't very comfortable with it, though. It just felt a little too … organic.

My brother, Michael, was a snurfer dude. Even after busting his skull on a metal fence post in Jeff Miller's back yard, he waxed up that board and went snurfing every time it snowed.

I bring this up because, of those three staples of 1960s suburbia, only the snurfer has survived. And it did so by adapting to a rapidly changing childhood recreational environment. In this case, the adaptation was driven by Jake Burton Carpenter, who invented the world's first snowboard by tweaking the snurfer. And then he went out and created the world's first demand for snowboards.

First, he cajoled local ski resorts into opening their lifts to "snowboarders" to increase awareness and demand. Then he sold snowboards at the nascent National Snowboarding Championships to increase sales and brand awareness. Then, to own the market, he bought the National Snowboarding Championships and turned it into the world renowned Burton US Snowboarding Championships. You see the trend.

Carpenter built his snowboard empire by telling people why they want a polyurethane-coated hunk of wood. It's not enough to have a good product, a dependable service, or a vital mission. To thrive in the Interactive Age, you must communicate the story behind the great product to build emotional connections with your audience.

3) Plan Ahead

Many organizations have a rather haphazard approach to social media, and this lack of clarity hinders their ability to tell their story. No matter which department or person formally "owns" social media, it's important to create social media guidelines in advance and disseminate them to everyone involved. Here are some of the areas that you should address:

"Lawn Darts! Culling the weak and slow from suburban neighborhoods since 1963."

- What topics and issues are not to be addressed?
- What sources or points of view are compatible with those of your organization?
- Guidelines for joking, using puns, *etc.*
- Protocols for dealing with complaints and criticisms
- Who can approve "gray area" posts?
- Who has authorization to post on the organization's behalf?
- Protocols for changing passwords if there is a security breach or staff turnover.

4) Develop a "crisis contingency plan"

Regardless of the event, there should be a plan in place to ensure that the relevant powers that be are informed as quickly as possible and that the organization is able to take action swiftly. So for all of your organization's areas or issues, answer the following questions:

- What is the "chain of command" for responding to new developments for this issue? This may be topically-based, for instance with the head of government affairs approving posts related to legislative developments. Or you may decide to have one person in charge of handling all communications crises.
- If one or more of the links in the chain are missing (on vacation, MIA, *etc.*), are there alternate people who can take their place? If not, who can be "deputized" to act on their behalf in these situations?
- Does everyone in this chain have the ability to reach everyone else swiftly? Do they all have each other's cell numbers, for instance?
- What is an acceptable turnaround time for developing and publicizing your reaction?

Stick a deadline on it

Accomplishing important tasks like this can be difficult when you're constantly swamped with more urgent issues. One of the best ways to get important but not urgent projects done is to assign it a deadline *and then tell someone who will hold you accountable for getting it done.*

Tips

- **Create a content stash.** Reviews of relevant books, quotes, and advice are all samples of the material you can put into your slush fund.

> **32** **Keep a content "slush fund" of evergreen blog and social media posts that you can easily load up when the unexpected gets thrown your way.**

- **Keep the end in mind.** You're probably not communicating just to check a box, so let your end goals guide when and where you post. If you care about Google search rankings, then you should care about regularly updating your Google+ page. It's usually better to pursue a focused outreach effort on the number of platforms that you can manage rather than post identical material across every platform you can think of.
- **Expect variation.** The time of year, time zone changes or sports events are amongst the many things that can change when and where people are online. Keep abreast of when these events are occurring and adjust accordingly.

Tools

- Scheduling and management tools like Hootsuite or Buffer are great ways to not only pre-load content but also to experiment with sending it out at different times.
- News aggregation services often come with a social media posting function. Paper.li, for instance, allows you to set up automatic daily tweets to let people know that there's a new edition of your "paper." It's an easy way to auto-pilot a daily supplement to your social media presence.

- If you are regularly posting to your blog, you might want to use a service like Dlvr.it to automatically share new posts across your social media platforms. This ensures that your generated content is consistently disseminated. If you do not want to automate it, make sure to have a checklist of the different platforms that should be sharing your blog updates. It's easy to forget one or two in the midst of a hectic day/week/month.

Why? Measuring and understanding social media success

One of the most common social media traps that people fall into is confusing action with results.

33 **Posting is not an end in and of itself ... nor is the number of followers you have, how often you post, or how many platforms you are using.**

Just like a TV show, you must always keep the end in mind. After all, TV shows aren't created for the fun of it, nor is the end product the number of people watching. The goal is to make money—through advertising sales, licensing agreements, *etc.*

So while it can be intoxicating to have a leap in your number of followers, you've got to keep your eye on the ultimate goal. And that's where analytics come in. They will help you track your actual progress towards reaching your goals.

Strategies and Tactics

1) Know what you're measuring and set up key performance indicators (KPIs) to determine the success or failure for your initiative.

Depending on your goal, it may be easy or nearly impossible to measure your progress. Developing a plan for what you are trying to achieve, which metrics indicate success, and the relative weight that each should be given in evaluating and refining activities can help you stay on track. Are you trying to get people to see your information, or are you trying to spark conversations around it? Are you trying to increase the number of unique visitors to your site, or to increase the overall number of visits that are made (including those made repeatedly by the same visitor)? You need targets and goals to help gauge the success of your efforts, and a set of metrics to help you correct course when necessary.

2) Make it routine

With such a focus on generating and curating content, analysis can easily fall by the wayside. Unfortunately, this is a bit like focusing on running as fast as you can but not paying attention to where you're heading.

Building regular reports or meetings—be they weekly, monthly, or quarterly—is a great way to improve the amount of intel, targeting, and accountability you receive.

3) Experiment, learn, and innovate

Given the accelerating acceleration of information-based and technological advancements, you can't afford to get complacent. This includes the analytics that you use to measure the results of your storytelling, and you may need to keep track of several different analytical programs to compile the overall information that you need.

Tips

- **"You can't manage what you don't measure."** This old management chestnut particularly applies to the quickly evolving social media world. Identify as many relevant metrics as possible that precede or indicate movement towards your ultimate goal.
- **Use A-B testing.** Use your analytics to test variations on timing, content, tone, *etc.* Small differences in text or layout can have a significant impact on how others perceive your message, and by comparing two different approaches you can measure how each is performing.

Tools

- If driving traffic to your website is a goal, tools like Google Analytics can give you intel on who is visiting your site, which pages they are viewing, how long they are staying, *etc.*

- In assessing reputation and influence, scoring programs like klout and kred can give you general indications of how your work is progressing.

- Most social media management tools have analytics functions, which you can use to get specific information on platform or program performance, as well as aggregating it to create a more holistic picture of your storytelling efforts

Conclusion

When the first portable cell phones came out a lot of people wondered just how rich you had to be to own one.

> And how strong you had to be to lug that monster around with you.

When Apple introduced the "home computing system," people asked why anyone would ever need a computer in their home.

And when the word "Facebook" dropped into our lexicon seemingly overnight, many adults dismissed it as "some new, complicated thing that the kids are getting into."

But the cell phone, PC, and Facebook are as much a part of your life as your television set is, more so if you've already cut the cable cord and now watch your shows on a tablet.

> If you haven't yet, just wait. You will.

And people generally don't think twice before tweeting, posting, Skyping, pinning, or otherwise sharing information with friends and family around the world.

> You've probably even forgotten that you used to have to pay *plenty* to make a long-distance phone call.

Well, very soon you will be systematically developing, managing, and distributing your organization's story online and measuring the impact that content is having on your audiences every day.

> Just like with the cell phone, PC, and social media, the seemingly daunting challenge of telling your organization's story will be as natural as checking in with your friends on Facebook.

As natural, perhaps, but it will require teamwork and planning since you're telling your *organization's* story, not just your own. And that's why approaching this new communication paradigm as if you were producing a TV show will be so helpful.

But as we said from the start, this book was designed to help you rethink how you approach organization storytelling online. There are countless bloggers, authors, and experts who can provide much greater depth to any one of the many facets of storytelling we have shared with you.

In no particular order, here are a few of our favorite websites. We strongly recommend that you check them out.

- www.contentmarketingin stitute.com

- http://www.annhandley. com/blog/

- http://winningthestoryw ars.com

- http://wiredforstory.co m/

- http://www.business2co mmunity.com

- http://socialmediatoday. com/

- http://bowden2bowden. co/

- http://digitalsherpa.com /blog/

And here are some brilliantly funny folks I like to check in with when my mind has slipped the leash and gone for a walkabout.

- www.xkcd.com – Simple, compelling graphics

- www.27bslash6.com/ -- Rich character development

- www.MariaBamford.com – Instructional use of video and a bipolar disorder

Last but certainly not least, please don't think that we practice all of these tips perfectly and consistently. Becoming the best storyteller possible is an ongoing and obstacle-filled journey. Visit DoyleMcDonald.com to join us on our quest, or just to share your comments, questions, critiques, and/or compliments.

We're right across the street from Mapquest, just a few blocks south of where Amazon and Gmail intersect. You can't miss it. We'll leave the light on for you.

Say "goodnight, John."

Goodnight, John.

TV Guides

1 The 20th century leadership skills that catapulted people to positions of power—being unilaterally decisive and hogging the megaphone, to name just two—are liabilities in the Interactive Age, where collaboration trumps intimidation.

2 The monolithic monologues that were the hallmark of "communication" in the 20th century have been replaced by countless dialogues— richer, more personal stories that are shared by smaller communities through an array of interactive media.

3 In using TV as your muse, the most important element is the inherent and ongoing relationship the audience has with your "show."

4 Familiarity is comforting. Repetition is not. A loyal TV audience keeps coming back because they want to know "what happens next." Same goes for your online followers. You need to keep the narrative flowing and to keep your stories fresh.

5 To keep their ratings (and their spirits) up, TV producers are doing what the most popular websites do: they're identifying very specific— and usually smaller—audiences that matter most, and they're tailoring their content to reach them.

6 You need to constantly monitor your site's data to see what works and what doesn't—and then adjust your content accordingly.

7 Just like a TV show, it takes regular and ongoing communications to make an organization's story come alive. This is not a "special project"; it is a new way of organizing and integrating your staffing to meet communications challenges that develop.

8 Social media has brought us full circle to what Bernays described as "an earlier age … [where] a leader was usually known to his followers personally [and] communication was accomplished principally by personal announcement to an audience."

9 Today, the value of information is not predicated on how much people are willing to pay to receive it. It is determined by how many people want to share it.

10 As people are sifting through huge quantities of information, it is the small, catchy "essence" that will cause them to pause.

11 One way to facilitate communication among very different communities is to spell out the assumptions and beliefs that are behind any given conclusion.

12 Your audience is no longer a passive group that enters into your situational construct. They react, interpret, and change it—even as you first produce it and long after you've moved on to other projects.

13 While there's value in sharing your accomplishments, there's less need (and less benefit) in tooting your own horn than in previous times. You still discuss your activities, of course. You just do so more gracefully and subtly than before.

14 Instead of blindly accepting the sales pitches of corporations, people are making purchasing decisions based on their beliefs and experiences with a given company.

15 It doesn't matter if you're selling a product, providing a service, or advancing an idea, success today depends on doing work that reflects your values—and conveying those values to your audience through stories.

16 When you connect with your core audience and share with them the passion you have for the work your organization does, you will inspire them to join you in your quest.

17 The *story* is neither solely about your quest nor your audience, but rather how your audience perceives and interacts with your quest.

18 Conflict is an essential part of every story. A story without conflict is propaganda.

19 With about 65 percent of the population being visual learners, "location shots" are an effective form of shorthand for communicating themes and reminding viewers of underlying beliefs and assumptions woven into the show.

20 Webinars, Skype, Vine, and other video platforms demand human involvement.

21 Simplifying your language, making it more enjoyable through rhyming or alliteration, and communicating clearly all help to make your story more credible.

22 If you lie, you *will* be caught. And once you're caught, expect not only an immediate negative backlash but also a long-term reduction in credibility.

23 "No comment" is no longer an option. If the story is about you, you have to be a part of it. You cannot let others tell your story for you.

24 If you want people to listen to your story, you must hit them with your best information immediately.

25 Brevity is the soul of wit. The two most important elements of any story are the beginning and the end. The closer together you put these two critical elements, the better your story will be.

26 Great storytelling, like great dancing, is an art that requires an almost spiritual connection with your partner, the audience.

27 Preparation increases your chances of communicating effectively.

28 Your audience is looking at your clothes, posture, and facial expressions. And they are making judgments about you, your issue, and your organization based on what they see.

29 Making an effort to create an outfit that supports your persona will help you get in character while also lending a visual interpretation of the personality you're trying to convey.

30 The days of talking *to* are over. You now must communicate *with* your partners, honestly and transparently.

31 It is incumbent on your organization to remain on top of current events, developments in your industry, and to keep a finger on the pulse of what people are saying about your organization on social media platforms.

32 Keep a content "slush fund" of evergreen blog and social media posts that you can easily load up when the unexpected gets thrown your way.

33 Posting is not an end in and of itself ... nor is the number of followers you have, how often you post, or how many platforms you are using.

ABOUT THE AUTHORS

Megan McDonald co-founded Doyle McDonald, a consulting firm that specializes in helping organizations tell their story more effectively. By the age of 28, she had already graduated *cum laude* from Yale, run a trade association and a nonprofit, and managed an international pro-democracy conference in Prague featuring then-President George W. Bush, former Czech Republic President Vaclav Havel, Presidential Medal of Freedom winner Natan Sharansky, and World Chess Champion Garry Kasparov.

Since then, she has advised the CEO's and other C-suite executives of Fortune 100 companies, domestic and international nonprofits, and small businesses on how to navigate the Interactive Age; completed her MSc in Comparative Politics from the London School of Economics; and visited as many countries as possible. She currently lives in Seattle with Phillip Johnny Bob and Wendell, her two cats.

John Doyle started talking professionally at age 12 when he landed the role of the Artful Dodger on one of the countless (and boring) "educational" television series that were big in the 70's. He sharpened his storytelling skills while bartending his way through college. And he learned the value of keeping his mouth shut while loading ships in North Jersey.

He started his grown-up career as a newspaper reporter, but left the Fourth Estate to pursue a profession that allowed him to tell stories more creatively. In his role as a DC flack, he developed and managed communications strategies for national trade associations, leading charities, and Fortune 100 companies. He has appeared frequently on the leading national news programs and talk shows—from CNN's *Crossfire* to Comedy Central's *Daily Show*. He is also the man behind the FlackOps.com curtain, which is currently read in 77 countries.

www.ingramcontent.com/pod-product-compliance
Lightning Source LLC
Chambersburg PA
CBHW060043210326
41520CB00009B/1248